EXPLORING DIGITAL TECHNOLOGY IN EDUCATION

Why Theory Matters and What to Do about It

Michael Hammond

D1612914

P

First published in Great Britain in 2023 by

Policy Press, an imprint of
Bristol University Press
University of Bristol
1–9 Old Park Hill
Bristol
BS2 8BB
UK
t: +44 (0)117 374 6645
e: bup-info@bristol.ac.uk

Details of international sales and distribution partners are available at
policy.bristoluniversitypress.co.uk

© Bristol University Press 2023

British Library Cataloguing in Publication Data
A catalogue record for this book is available from the British Library

ISBN 978-1-4473-6261-6 hardcover
ISBN 978-1-4473-6262-3 paperback
ISBN 978-1-4473-6263-0 ePub
ISBN 978-1-4473-6264-7 ePdf

Cover design: Hayes Design and Advertising
Front cover image: iStock/.shock
Bristol University Press and Policy Press use environmentally responsible print partners.
Printed and bound in Great Britain by CPI Group (UK) Ltd, Croydon, CR0 4YY

FSC
www.fsc.org
MIX
Paper | Supporting
responsible forestry
FSC® C013604

Contents

List of figures, tables and cases

Figures

Tables

Cases

Preface

This book is about theorising technology and education and how we can theorise better. It will be particularly valuable for those interested in researching the ways in which technology has influenced teaching and learning – across different sectors and in both formal and informal settings. However, it will also have a more general appeal to those interested in, and perhaps flummoxed by, the idea of theory, in respect to education and social research in general.

The aim of the book is then to clarify the idea of theory and to encourage researchers to be more theoretical. I am interested in promoting discussion of theory and while I provide a clear agenda for how we can theorise better, this is not a 'how to research' guide. Moreover, my aim is to promote theorising, not a particular theoretical framework or theory. At this point, I do recognise that there are plenty of books on technology and digital tools in and beyond the classroom and for that matter several books on theory and theorising, so why another one? I have three main objectives.

First, I want to show that theory need not be so mystifying a concept if we think about it in broad and inclusive ways. Theory comes with many different associations, but at heart it is about providing an explanation, not any explanation but one that is backed up using concepts and ideas from a wider field of study. This is not difficult to understand even if discussion of theory is often emotionally charged. It is, after all, a major put-down to be told that our work is lacking theory or that we have misunderstood theory X or theory Y. Yet those who are so eager to critique the theoretical efforts of others often believe that theirs is the only legitimate version of theory and fail to set out what they mean by theory in the first place. We should not let that put us off offering theoretical claims of our own and doing so on our own terms.

Second, there have been strong criticisms of research into technology and education and a perceived lack of theoretical rigour within the field. Researchers have been criticised for superficiality, for being guided by novelty, and for offering romanticised accounts of technology. I accept some of this, but I want to use the book to offer a more balanced view of the field.

Third, technology is routinely described as 'new' but its use in education goes back decades. For those that care to look, there is a long history of experiments with technology for learning, taking in educational radio and television, tape recordings, old-style projection devices and so on. Indeed, there is a rich history of the use of computers themselves with terminals introduced into some schools as long ago as the 1970s and the microcomputer taking off in many schools in the 1980s. I want to show the importance of looking back on what has gone on earlier. If we do not do this then we have missed opportunities to theorise and to write about technology in a more critical way.

Structure of the book

The book is organised around seven chapters. Each chapter begins with a brief signpost to what is covered and how the chapter fits the overarching flow of the book. Chapters end with a summary and suggestions for further reading. Sections are, wherever helpful, illustrated using examples to draw attention to strengths or shortcomings in a particular research tradition. Longer case studies are also supplied to show a research approach in more depth. The studies I cite take in different contexts, though there is probably more on schools as this is where some of the debates have been most vigorous. Some of the studies are more convincing than others, but I have tried not to include too much which is obviously methodologically flawed. This does not stop me making forceful criticisms at times.

Chapter 1 sets the book in motion by asking 'What is theory?'. I look at several associations made with the word. For some, theory is about uncovering causal relationships between variables X (for example, technology) and Y (learning outcomes) or modelling the various factors that combine to produce an outcome. A different theoretical goal, particularly in qualitative research, may be putting forward a new concept (for example, 'online presence') to capture a phenomenon and charting the consequences of this phenomenon for teaching and learning. Theory can also be normative (what ought to happen) and theory in the field of education often has an action orientation that sets it apart from social science. We can then see theory in all aspects of social research but if there is one recurring idea about theory it is that of providing an explanation and different kinds of explanations are discussed. I finish the chapter by looking at criticisms of research into technology in education and asking are these criticisms fair?

If theory is a difficult term then theorising is no easier. In Chapter 2 I see theorising as associated with a move from descriptive to more explanatory reporting. So far, so good. However, explanations come in different shapes and sizes and I am particularly interested in theoretical explanation that draws on subject knowledge – of course subject knowledge of technology in education, but also of education and social research in general. The work of theorising may be undertaken in a step-by-step manner but it often involves a leap of imagination too, enabling the researcher to see the data in a new and more coherent way. These leaps of the imagination, often described as abduction or guesswork, are difficult to describe and cannot be legislated for, but they do not come out of nothing. They are products of an intense engagement with the concepts and approaches researchers have read and thought about over the course of their project. Thus, a good place to start if we are to theorise better is to explore the concepts and vocabulary we have inherited in the field of technology and education. Of course, not everything can be covered but in the following three chapters I look at research on: learning and technology; teachers and technology; and technology itself. I show how theoretical approaches have been employed in these areas and how they have sharpened our thinking.

Chapter 3 focuses on learning and technology and looks at learning theory. I go back to 'traditional' learning theories of behaviourism, cognitivism and social constructionism as associated with Vygotsky before looking at social theories of learning, including community of practice, and examples of distributed learning specific to technology mediation. Theories of learning work by focusing attention on what is important and help both the researcher and practitioner make sense of an otherwise overwhelming context. However, theories come with shortcomings and some are tempted to claim that advances in learning analytics and artificial intelligence have obviated the need for theory given the sheer quantity of data that can be drawn on and the speed with which these data can be processed. It is a view that I critique.

Chapter 4 looks at schools and teachers and their use of technology. Here is a paradox. Computers can offer powerful support for learning but even when problems of access have been addressed the take-up of technology has often disappointed. Teachers often say they are keen to use technology and in many countries will use digital devices in their personal lives, but they seem reluctant to use it in the classroom. Why is this? Tyack and Cuban (1995), in an influential contribution, explained that technology did not seem to fit the 'grammar of schooling'; teachers were constrained by the curriculum they had to get through and the pattern of the school day. Since interventions by Tyack, Cuban and others we now have more social psychology approaches, such as ecological theory, and sociology approaches, such as activity theory, on which to draw. These approaches show how teachers' work is embedded in wider systems that constrain their actions and, at their best, allow us to see opportunities for change.

Chapter 5 goes into the theorisation of technology itself. Here there is another paradox: researchers interested in technology and education have not always had a lot to say about technology itself. Rather there has been a technocentric tradition which has tended to assume tools will be used as intended by designers and teaching experts across different contexts. Of course, this is not the whole story and I look at alternative ways of conceptualising technology, including the idea of affordances as first put forward by Gibson. I then go on to look at efforts to see technology use in hybrid and ecological contexts, and this takes us into the language of assemblage, that is, networks of people and artefacts. I look too at ways in which technology use is shaped by social and commercial forces before finally considering more action-oriented approaches, including participatory design and design thinking.

Having looked at some of the debates about technology, and its use in teaching and learning, I turn in Chapter 6 to wider narratives about technology itself. Here there is both excessive optimism and pessimism about the impact of technology and this is distorting the discussion of digital tools in school and beyond. I argue for a more balanced view which better accounts for the context in which technology is used and acknowledges the different ways that technology is experienced by users. Moreover, there is something inherent in the technology which means it offers both opportunity and constraint, rather than easy answers. An important question is not whether technology is in itself an asset for teaching and learning, but how can we use technology for desirable educational ends.

Finally, in Chapter 7 I reprise some of the key arguments made in the book and suggest we need a research community which values different kinds of theoretical contribution, while maintaining a distinctive focus on education. This community will consider what is new, but will use the past as a guide to the present. Community members will be enthused about technology but will not be afraid of standing on the sidelines and reminding anyone who cares to listen that claims for the impact of technology are often overstated and go unfulfilled. I then finish the chapter by suggesting ways in which individual researchers may theorise better in their own work. Theory is important, as without theoretical insight we are left to the whims of what is most novel or most touted by vested interests and/or policy makers. Theory is for everyone.

This book draws on work in technology research that I have carried out over the years and I would like to thank colleagues in the education research community for sharing their ideas with me. I was also fortunate to work with Cristina Costa and Sarah Younie on a special edition of theorising technology for the journal *Technology Pedagogy and Education*. I was given a grant from the University of Warwick Institute of Advanced Teaching and Learning fund to develop a small project on theorising and would like to thank the colleagues and research students who contributed to this project. Thank you, too, to Penny Nunn for reading and re-reading the text so thoroughly. Although they are unlikely ever to read it, the book is nonetheless dedicated to Alfie, Clara, Emmeline, Orrin and Wilf for finding their voices in an increasingly technological world.

All errors and gaps in understanding are my own responsibility.

1

What is theory?

If we are looking at the question 'How can we theorise better?', then we need to start by looking at the idea of theory. In fact theory is a slippery concept. So what then is theory? I address this and other questions in the following sections:

- What is the problem with theory?
- How theory appears in different types of research
- What is a theoretical contribution and are we making one?

What is the problem with theory?

The problem with discussing theory is that many of us have different ideas as to what theory is and rather than get to the root of these differences we end up avoiding discussion of theory altogether. Thus, the request to be more theoretical in an article, thesis or dissertation can cause unease, even panic, especially for those in practice disciplines such as education. Kiley illustrates this point by citing a doctorate student looking back on the experience of being examined in a viva: 'people kept asking me about my theoretical perspective, but I didn't have a clue what they were talking about' (2015: 57).

Rather than being flummoxed by the request for theoretical insight, we could, of course, reject such a request as out of order. After all, most of us who see ourselves as part of an education research community accept the idea that our work should be practical and inform practice, rather than address theoretical questions. To back this up, there is a long tradition that argues what matters to the practitioner is not formal knowledge of teaching, but practical know-how, in particular an understanding of what to do in a new situation by calling up, and reflecting on, past experience. Moreover, the search for theoretical alignment can seem off-putting or even dangerous as it appears all-encompassing. For example, practitioners fear being characterised as aligned to cognitivist, social constructivist or behaviourist positions as they know that their practice is varied and what they do in the classroom is tailored to circumstance. To the extent that practitioners are interested in wider exploration of their practice they might be just as influenced by metaphors around teaching (Shulman, 1986), or by narratives and 'folk pedagogy' (Bruner, 2020), as much as by formal theory (for example, the learning theory of Skinner, Piaget and Vygotsky). There is an artistry about knowledge-in-action that those over-committed to producing formal theories of education do not see. Carr and Kemmis, in talking about action research, make the point that: 'At the outset, then, it is important to recognise that [the] testing ground for educational research is not its theoretical sophistication or its ability to conform to criteria derived from the social sciences, but rather its capacity to resolve educational problems and improve educational practice' (Carr and Kemmis, 1986: 109). Many would agree with Carr and Kemmis even if they are not action researchers themselves.

Scepticism about theory is often shared by policy makers looking for 'what works' accounts of the impact of their interventions rather than theoretical contributions (Biesta, 2010). I have previously drawn on an apocryphal story of a minister in the French government, a minister of education:

> One day a civil servant proudly brings him (it is a 'him' in this case) a solution to a problem, an apparently intractable problem that has dogged French education for a great many years. The minister looks at the plan unenthusiastically, coughs loudly and mutters, 'Yes, that is all very well, but I am sorry can you tell me how all this works in theory?'. The story is sometimes told in support of a more applied Anglo-Saxon research tradition, rather than a French tradition, in which theorising, at least in the view of its critics, is carried out for its own sake. Too much theory, it is implied can lead you into philosophical speculation and away from findings common sense solutions. (Hammond and Wellington, 2019: 81)

Yet I believe that theory does matter and often those who dismiss the contribution of theory carry a jaundiced view of what theory is. If we are to avoid dogmatism we need to have a broad and flexible concept of theory. For example, Carr and Kemmis are not saying we should forget all reference to social theory or why would they write an intensely theoretical book on education research, bringing in reference to social theorists such as Marx and Habermas for good measure? Theory can be practical and enlightening. And if we go to our fictional minister in France, perhaps he had a point: if a solution is to work we need to know why it will work. It has to have a theoretical basis otherwise we will not be able to learn from it or know how to adapt as circumstances change.

We should not, then, put a wall between theory and practice; one can inform the other. This becomes particularly important in the research of technology in education. This is a field in which large sums are invested in hardware and software and high hopes are generated by technology use. There is, consequently, a lot of implicit and explicit pressure on researchers to provide evidence of impact. But without a theoretical basis their reporting becomes piecemeal, almost random. We get interesting data but not a picture of how technology works or how we can transfer what we learn from one study to another. So how can we theorise better? To begin to find an answer we need first to take stock of the different meanings which have been attached to theory.

How theory appears in different types of research

We begin by looking at seven ways in which theory can make an appearance in research on the use of technology in education.

Type 1: A conceptualisation of a phenomenon

Here researchers are inviting us to look at an event or phenomenon in a particular way, often by introducing new and helpful concepts. A well-known example is the concept of technological pedagogical content knowledge (TPCK) (Mishra and Koehler, 2006). TPCK (alternatively, technological pedagogical *and* content knowledge, or TPACK) is the subject of much debate and, in view of later critical comments, I want to stress that it provides really helpful insight into teacher development. It does this by making the case that in order to use technology productively teachers should have knowledge of *technology* (for example, how to set up and control a Zoom meeting); knowledge of *pedagogy* (for example, how to set up and support online group discussion); *and* knowledge of the subject or *content* (for example, knowledge of fractions, language structures, forms or systems of government or whatever they are asked to teach). There should be an integration of these different types of knowledge so that technological knowledge is not out of kilter with pedagogical or content knowledge and training and development activities are not dominated by instructions on how to use the software. Of course, people had thought about different kinds of teacher knowledge long before encountering the concept of TPCK. However, with TPCK at the front of their thoughts, leaders could be encouraged to plan and design technology training in a more holistic manner (for example, Aggeliki et al, 2018) and better understand why training should focus on something more than the teaching of information technology (IT) skills.

A second example of a useful concept goes back to the early days of computers in school and a reflection by Olson (1988), following observation of teachers in a primary school in Canada, of the importance of 'familiar routines', defined as established ways for managing classroom interactions to enable both teachers and students to have experiences they value. Olson describes how teachers may see a new tool, the microcomputer, as potentially disruptive and something which they need to get under control.

Olson sees the need for routine as crucial for some teachers, for rather than being a block on creativity that proponents of technology-led change often assume, routines are necessary to make the job of teaching doable in the first place. Olson stresses that routines 'are not thoughtless or dull' (Olson, 1988: 90), they are ways of working that have been established over time. In contrast, those arguing for technology often associate its use with new kinds of pedagogy, leading to more exploratory learning ('the sage on the stage' to be replaced by 'the guide on the side'). However, such a change of role would, at least for one teacher in Olson's study, threaten his concept of teaching. This teacher needed to lead students in order to do his job properly, he needed to show students:

> [W]hat is important to learn, as well as helping them to learn it. He is able to do this [lead] because he knows how to diagnose learning difficulties and remedy them. Standing in the eyes of students depends on these abilities in order to be helpful he has to construe ambiguous classroom events quickly. (Olson, 1988: 4)

Olson's concept of familiar routine is a benign one, others may see the need to be in control in a different light. However, Olson helps us think about the role of teachers in a more rounded way and shows that there is more to teacher direction than meets the eye. He reminds us that teaching looks very different from the perspective of a teacher than the educational reformer.

Introducing concepts to the study of technology and education may seem a modest contribution, but these two examples show that it is not. Language shapes our thoughts and a great deal of work concerning technology has concerned itself with developing a new vocabulary to describe learning (for example, networked learning, computer support collaborative learning) and new phenomena (for example, online community, online presence, virtual worlds). These efforts can be described as theoretical contributions.

Type 2: Creating a typology or system of classification

A typology draws attention to what different people or different tools or different phenomena have, or do not have, in common. Typologies remind us that while we can ask about the effect of information and communications technology (ICT) on learning, it might be better to ask how particular kinds of tools work for particular learners rather than investigate impact in general (Passey, 2013).

Technology researchers have themselves developed many typologies, including ones covering teacher beliefs concerning technology (for example, Mama and Hennessy, 2013), students' motivation to use technology in learning (for example, Stevens et al, 2018), or, as in the following example taken from the early days of IT in schools, types of software. In this example, MacDonald (1977) and colleagues saw three (plus one) 'paradigms' of software design, paraphrased here:

- The instructional paradigm. This was strongly associated with drill-and-practice programmes which provide automated feedback (that is, reinforcement of successful responses/correction of wrong response) for discrete items of knowledge.
- The revelatory paradigm. This covered simulation packages and some kinds of data-handling programmes. Here designers and programmers worked with a 'model of reality' that they hoped the user would comprehend through experimentation and reflection. An example might be a roller coaster simulation (there are several available on the web) in which users can alter variables, such as gravity at work, mass of car and size of loops in the track, in order to gain an understanding of physical forces. Using the simulation, the user might be asked to produce as exciting a ride as possible without the car falling off the track.
- The conjectural paradigm. This shares with the revelatory paradigm a concern for experimentation but here the user can create their own products rather than try to unpick the model that the designer had in mind. A classic example would be Logo, which allows learners to construct their own designs by getting immediate feedback on their programming statements.

The 'plus one' in this typology is the emancipatory or labour-saving paradigm. An example of this would be the use of computer-generated graphical displays to cut out the labour of producing graphs by hand, leaving more time for developing the higher order skill of data analysis. More recently, the idea of a flipped classroom follows a similar emancipatory logic. Here, lower-level grafting can be undertaken remotely, say, by following online lectures and taking interactive quizzes. This would free up classroom learning to be reserved for higher-level discussion of concepts and collaboration, for which teacher mediation is essential (Akçayır and Akçayır, 2018). Saving time and cutting out what is sometimes called 'inauthentic work' (for example, carrying out complex calculations 'by hand' without a calculator or spreadsheet) is a key goal of all computer programmes but defining what is inauthentic for particular learners in and out of the classroom is, of course, a matter for debate.

A second example of a classification system is provided by Agudo-Peregrina et al (2014), who point to the mass of data generated within a virtual learning environment (VLE). Drawing on the literature they suggest classifying interactions according to:

- Agent: here they look at student–student, student–teacher and student–content interaction.

- Frequency of use: features of the VLE which are most used, moderately used and rarely used.
- Style of participation: active (for example, posting a message); passive (for example, reading a message) tasks.

Using such a classification system they are able to draw conclusions not so much about activity in general, but about particular types of activity. Moreover, typologies such as these can be used by other researchers and enable a narrative around online learning to build up. Typologies sensitise other researchers as to what to look for, but no typology should be set in stone. Other researchers might end up adapting an existing typology or offering a new one of their own.

For some commentators, typologies and classifications can appear quite flat and descriptive, not theoretical at all. However, they can be used in more analytical ways. For example, MacDonald (1977) and colleagues were able to match each typology to types of learning interaction and take a step towards a theory of computer-based learning and Agudo-Peregrina et al (2014) suggest that there is a relationship between particular types of interaction and better academic performance.

Type 3: Providing a conceptual framework or model

Conceptual frameworks or models provide a way of presenting the key variables in a study and how these variables fit together to produce certain outcomes. They are often presented in the form of a diagram or map and are labelled as theories in that they provide explanations for actions and events.

In the context of digital technology one very well-used model is Davis's (1989) technology acceptance model (TAM), as shown in Figure 1.1. The origins of TAM lie in earlier research by Fishbein and Ajzen (1980) and

Figure 1.1: A technology acceptance model

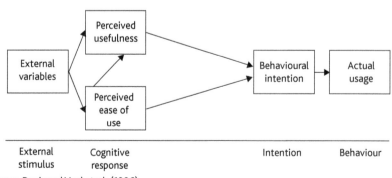

Source: Davis and Venkatesh (1996)

6

their theory of reasoned action (TRA). TRA had at its heart the idea that intention is the best indicator of behaviour, that is, if we want to do something we will do it. This is intuitive as an idea and TRA has been used in a raft of contexts including studies of organisations, consumer behaviour and adapted in research on technology take-up. Of course, there is more at stake when trying to understand decision making and reasoned action will be influenced by how we feel about certain behaviour (for example, whether we are risk-takers), and what others think about the decisions we are making. Critically, we will be influenced by whether or not we believe our decisions will actually result in the outcomes we had hoped for.

Davis (1989) drew on TRA and other models to address the issue of how and why some users come to accept a technology and others do not. In particular, he saw behavioural intention, and hence actual usage, as influenced by two key perceptions: perceived usefulness (PU) and perceived ease of use (PE). In other words is it worthwhile to spend time and effort learning to use a new tool? The answer may well be 'yes' if the tool enables us to do the job better and it is relatively easy to learn to use. Technology acceptance, however, does not take place in a vacuum and, as with TRA, TAM brings external variables into the model (Davis and Venkatesh, 1996).

The TAM model can be used in two ways. The first is the more usual deductive approach in which researchers start with a commitment to a model and seek to assess its validity in a new context (for example, Fianu et al, 2020). If taking this approach researchers should, of course, explain why they are using TAM in the first place, and not any alternative model. They should then set about operationalising the key variables, in other words producing or accessing reliable inventories to measure PU and PE and define what they mean by technology take-up behaviour. The deductive approach is then asking 'Does the TAM successfully predict who uses technology and who does not?'. If it does not, then the model should be amended in the light of the data.

TAM can, however, be used in a more inductive, or at least in a more flexible, way. Rather than being over-committed to TAM in the first place this could be one of several theories that helps orient a researcher in studying ICT take-up in a new context and may, later on, help contribute to an explanation for findings within a study (see Batane and Ngwako, 2017). There is, in fact, a strong case for using TAM flexibly as Davis and collaborators have themselves re-worked the model over time. Adaption seems especially important as TAM was generated to explain technology take-up in commercial, not educational, settings.

Models are often seen as belonging to a more quantitative tradition but qualitative researchers may produce formal models of their own. In one study Morris and Cravens Pickens (2017) looked at the consequences of 'unplugging' (completely disconnecting from certain types of technology or digital media) for well-being and relationships. Using 29 publicly shared stories on blogs, websites and news articles, the authors present a theoretical model using grounded theory methodology. The model includes four thematic codes: *taking the initial steps; realising the dependence; regaining time and life; re-plugging and evaluating the experience* (see Figure 1.2). The value of the model is that it shows the process of unplugging, from the perspective of those suspending use of technology, and how each stage flows into the next. The model looks useful for sensitising researchers of unplugging as to what to look for, but it is not pre-ordained that anyone unplugging in the future would go through the same process as reported here. This is important to stress as there is always a danger that models will be over-interpreted.

Type 4: Testing a hypothesis in experimental conditions

In everyday contexts when we say we have a theory about something we are referring to a belief that we have an explanation that will work. This intuitive idea is carried over when setting out a hypothesis within the experimental method. This aligns closely to the deductive approach mentioned earlier but here a theory is tested by asking whether those who get an intervention (say, access to technology) achieve better measurable outcomes (say, higher test scores) than those that do not.

An example of the experimental approach is Kang and Zhang (2020) who explore whether online forums can act as a complement to face-to-face (F2F) teaching with the goal of improving student motivation and engagement. The authors believed that such forums could provide engaging learning environments, a 'third space' in which communication and collaboration could happen 'anytime and anywhere'. This belief was tested in the context of an intervention in higher education in which students who had access to an online teaching forum (a supplement to regular class teaching) were compared to those who did not. The authors' concern was not to measure assessment outcomes but the more complex issues of engagement and motivation, something they evaluated through homework assignment data and student surveys. They concluded that forums were indeed helpful in addressing procrastination and plagiarism and their hypothesis was confirmed.

The impact of interventions can be explored more generally by reviewing past studies, not just by carrying out a one-off intervention. A systematic review does this by using objective criteria for deciding which studies to include. For example, Akçayır and Akçayır (2018), cited earlier in the context of the flipped classroom, accessed appropriate studies by carrying out keyword searches within journals that had passed a quality threshold. All studies meeting their criteria had to be included to provide a higher level of objectivity.

Figure 1.2: A four-stage model of unplugging

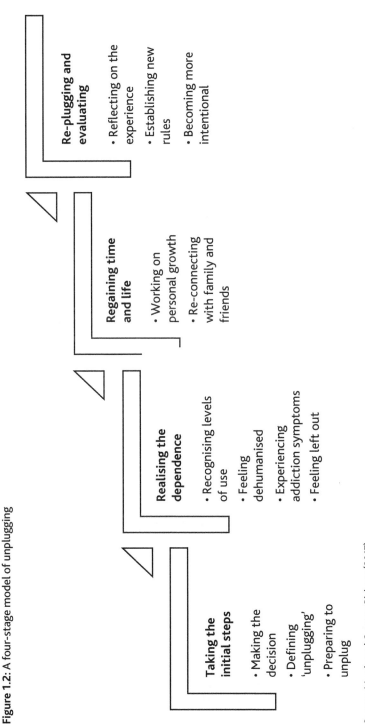

Taking the initial steps
- Making the decision
- Defining 'unplugging'
- Preparing to unplug

Realising the dependence
- Recognising levels of use
- Feeling dehumanised
- Experiencing addiction symptoms
- Feeling left out

Regaining time and life
- Working on personal growth
- Re-connecting with family and friends

Re-plugging and evaluating
- Reflecting on the experience
- Establishing new rules
- Becoming more intentional

Source: Morris and Cravens Pickens (2017)

A particular kind of systematic review seeks to aggregate the learning gains from solely experimental method studies in order to reach a general conclusion. An example of such an approach covers the use of immersive reality in teaching and learning (Hamilton et al, 2021). The authors examined studies published since 2013, in order to assess whether students using head mounted display (HMD) based interactive video had better assessment outcomes compared to those accessing less immersive tools such as desktop computers and slideshows. They used objective criteria for accessing publications and found 29 suitable studies. The value of virtual reality was shown in that most, though by no means all, cases students using HMD achieved better outcomes. However, the authors question the reliability of the studies as they often concerned brief interventions testing short-term recall, and were reporting on a small number of contexts. Thus, systematic reviews provide a very useful overview of a field of research, but they are dependent on researchers having access to a decent number of high-quality papers. They can make a theoretical contribution by going beyond a description of findings and showing how variables and outcomes are related.

Type 5: An experiment with technology

Rather than carry out a full-on experimental study some researchers carry out shorter experiments in teaching to address a problem or opportunity in practice. Much action research has this experimental character. Here practitioner researchers may be influenced by previous work in their field, but typically they are prepared to jettison one theory for another if that is where their intervention leads them. Most action researchers would probably add that they are aiming to create solutions to local problems rather than trying to contribute to a general theory.

Pitura and Terlecka-Pacut (2018) provide an example. They review the literature and explain that they wanted to see if technology-assisted urban games had the potential to help address language curriculum challenges in Poland. They devised tasks that led students to explore historical locations in the city of Cracow, and, in some cases, prompted them to interview English-speaking overseas tourists. Students later returned to school and used the material they had amassed for creating multimedia online presentations in English. The authors felt that they had shown that students could carry out authentic language tasks, supported by ICT.

In a second example, Supriyadi et al (2020) were worried about how access to the internet was making it possible for learners to access false *hadith*s (in the Islamic tradition a hadith is a saying which offers guidance on personal conduct ultimately seen as deriving from the prophet Muhammad). The researchers' intervention was aimed at supporting students' literacy skills so that these students would be better able to trace the authenticity of a hadith. They provided evidence that the intervention was successful, leading to improvements in 'data literacy, technological literacy, and human literacy related to narration of the hadith'. As with Pitura and Terlecka-Pacut, Supriyadi et al's reporting is heavy on description and light on theory, but both papers highlight what is important in their interventions and how successful outcomes were achieved.

Type 6: A perspective on what ought to be

Most educational research sets out implications for practice, but some theoretical contributions embrace this challenge more than others. Typically, those focusing on what ought to happen have organising principles of teaching, perhaps an 'ideal state of teaching with technology', with which they want to compare practice. A recent example is Mogas et al (2022). Here the authors suggest there have been successive industrial revolutions which bring under-explored opportunities to schools:

> Since the eighteenth century, consecutive industrial revolutions allowed huge improvements in manufacturing and mass production thanks to cast iron production, steam engines, advances in the textile industry, combustion engines, and electricity. The Third Industrial Revolution arrived in the decade of 1980 thanks to the popularisation of electronic devices such as personal computers, telecommunication, and developments in computer science. Nowadays, evolution is becoming more complex and merges physical reality with virtuality into a new conception of web-based cyber-physical interconnected systems (Ng, 2020; Zhong et al., 2017). This new paradigm shapes the Fourth Industrial Revolution (4IR) and brings unexplored possibilities in relation to educational automation and optimisation processes. Learning environments can be synchronous hybrid or blended, with both on-site and remote students interacting and participating in learning activities as if they are in the same place (Raes et al., 2019) and with all objects of the learning organisation being interconnected. (Mogas et al, 2022: 878)

The quote crystallises a simple intuitive idea about education: it does not keep up with what is happening in the world and really it should make more of an effort to do so. It is a theoretical contribution informed by value judgements about technology.

Prescriptive commentaries on the use of ICT are often optimistic, but some can be pessimistic, as in Kwet (2017). He argues that our understanding of technology is distorted by commercial interests and that policy makers can be naive as to its impact. The context being discussed was the introduction of programmes which would use learning analytics to develop education in South Africa. These programmes would allow each learner to work to a 'personalised' learning plan that could be derived by 'watching and recording nearly every aspect of a learner's digital activity'. Kwet (2017) focuses on several flaws in the use of analytics, homing in on the issue of surveillance:

> According to a large body of research, surveillance chills free speech and inquiry. Study after study shows individuals conform to the expectations of the status quo when they know they are being watched. It reasonable to expect that pervasive data collection will curb the speech, inquiry, and behaviour of learners and educators if they know their activity is under corporate and government surveillance. (Kwet, 2017: 11)

Here Kwet uses his knowledge of research, and his own experience of surveillance in the South African context, to draw attention to the dangers of handing over control of data to corporate interests. His is not so much a counter-view to Mogas et al's, in which risks of surveillance are also raised, but Kwet does start from a much greater degree of scepticism about technology.

Type 7: An analysis of key theorists and theories

Some researchers make a theoretical contribution by offering detailed analyses of relevant thinkers or earlier currents of thinking to draw out implications for contemporary research. For example, Hickman (2009) looks at the ways in which John Dewey's work can help us understand technology. He explains that Dewey saw learning as a 'transaction' between the person and the environment, that is, we learn through seeking to make sense of our environment using whatever tools are to hand. By tools Dewey is not just interested in material tools, but also abstract thought and cultural practices. Like all thinkers Dewey's work can be interpreted in different ways but Hickman shows us that we need to think about technology in the context of problem solving. And we need to recognise that the problems we face do not have fixed solutions, rather our solutions are 'provisional' and call for further moral, practical and ethical inquiry. It is not clear from the paper what this means in practice (Hickman is, after all, a philosopher rather than an educationalist) but it seems clear that we should not try to teach with or about technology without providing practical problems for which there are no simple solutions. Further, we should prompt wider debate about the consequences of technology use.

In a second example, Wajcman (2010) looks at feminist theories of technology, rather than at one particular thinker or theory. She notes that there is a change of tone when comparing contemporary (this was 2010 but the paper still feels relevant at the time of writing) and earlier feminist strands of thinking. Contemporary approaches focus on the 'mutual shaping' of gender and technology, while earlier contributions tended to see technology use (in particular who gets to use and design technology) as necessarily gendered and a reflection of gender divides in society. This is an important change of perspective as contemporary approaches avoid what the author describes as technological determinism (that is, technology causes something to happen) and gender essentialism (practices are inevitably distorted by gender). Wajcman argues for a feminist politics of technology as a contribution to achieving gender equality. Like Hickman, Wajcman's article is rather abstract but this allows access to a broader range of thinking about technology.

What is a theoretical contribution and are we making one?

We can see from these examples that researchers have different goals for their research and think about theory in different ways. Yet across all the examples of research given in this chapter, there is a common thread: researchers are trying to explain what is happening when technology is used. Their explanations are, of course, different in scope and in epistemological assumptions. Some explanations are couched in terms of causality (for example, perception of ease of use, and usefulness, determine a decision to use technology); some are modelling processes (for example, there are stages when experiencing unplugging); some are looking at the consequences of actions and beliefs (for example, the effect of 'familiar routines' in computer take-up). A further contrast is between those that are directly addressing problems of practice (for example, how to promote digital literacy) as against offering more conceptual understanding (for example, a feminist perspective on technology, or how to categorise software). Some are self-consciously setting out values and beliefs (for example, making the case to use technology more to keep up with changes in civil society, or for using it less because of the risk of excessive surveillance).

Explanation then takes on different forms but no matter in which form it comes it lies at the heart of social research; if we are claiming theoretical insight we are saying we know why something is happening (Martindale, 2013). Thus, we can contrast largely descriptive accounts (for example, teachers did not change their behaviour when interactive whiteboards [IWBs] were introduced) with explanatory ones (for example, teachers did not change their behaviour when IWBs were introduced *because* they were committed to an instructional style of teaching). However, theory cannot simply be synonymous with explanation, it offers something distinctive and I have the rest of the book to explore this further. But, I can already say, reflecting on the examples in the previous section, that a theory should enable the reader to do some important things, including to:

- See a situation in a new way, for example, to see that technology is grossly underused, or that teachers can be resistant to technology for good reasons. Theories can be strikingly new ('that was how it used to be, but with this new theory this is how it is now'), but, more modestly, a theoretical contribution might offer a refinement of an existing theory (for example, an adaption of TAM) or take a theory from another context (for example, a theory of surveillance) and put it into a new context (for example, learning analytics). Theoretical explanations should add to our perspective on, in our case technology, and help us understand more.

- Follow a logical train of reasoning. We can and do make all kinds of intuitive associations with technology but these can be quite superficial. For example, we may see a child ignoring all attempts at conversation and apparently lost in repeatedly pressing buttons on a small Kindle and conclude that technology is addictive. Conversely, we might see another child playing an online game, marvel at the multitasking going on and conclude that technology is inherently liberating and playful. Both arguments have some merit but a theoretical explanation must go beyond the immediate perception and offer something more rigorous and defensible. To different degrees, the papers I have discussed try to do this. Like any reader I have my own ideas on how convincing they are but I can see they are making arguments supported by data (in its broadest sense data could cover literature as well as observations, interviews, survey and so on) and showing how these data are relevant to their argument.

- Identify what is key in the explanation. Theories abstract out key variables or key phenomena and represent them in models, concepts, typologies and classifications so that they are transferable, or at least relatable, to other studies. This, as we discuss later, creates a dilemma as the more abstract the study (for example, Hickman and Wajcman earlier) the more the reader is left asking, 'Yes, but which contexts do the authors have in mind?'. Yet, the more descriptive the study (for example, Pitura and Terlecka-Pacut), the more difficult it is to identify how to apply the findings in other teaching contexts.

- Consider questions of ontology and epistemology. We have seen that some theories rest on the idea that there is causality in the social world, for example, in some way ease of use triggers an intention to use a tool, while other theories are more focused on agency (for example, Pitura and Terlecka-Pacut, 2018; Supriyadi et al, 2020) and suggest we create uses for technology ourselves.

Finally, a theoretical contribution should be seen as contributing to a field of research, something I have called, in very general terms, the field of technology and education research. Within the field researchers may take up wildly different positions but each shares a concern for what technology is, why it is used or not used, what its impact might be and so on.

Does research into technology and education meet the criteria set out here? In fact, many commentators (for example, Underwood, 2004; Oliver, 2011; Selwyn, 2011b; Bulfin et al, 2015; Drew and Mann, 2018) have put forward complaints about the state of technology in education research. These include:

- Research is piecemeal and overly descriptive. We might learn, for example, that students used a VLE for one thing and not another; teachers and students enjoyed communicating online but not synchronously; that some teachers used multiple-choice tests with one class but not another. As an analogy, it is as though researchers have produced phrase books that help us to get by when visiting a new country but have not developed a language with a common grammar and vocabulary to help us to think and write more deeply about technology.
- As researchers we run after novelty and are too eager to see technology as offering a clear break with the past. However, this stops us from building up a historically rich picture of technology and learning. For example, blended and mobile learning are new concepts but learning at a distance is age old and past experiences could provide useful insight. We seem to continually rebrand our work in the hope that earlier problems can be wiped clean.
- A lot of studies of technology are really rather dull. This need not be a criticism as academic research is, some would argue, necessarily austere and reserved; researchers are not writing novels. However, the problem is that many studies are flat, a theory should provide something insightful and fresh. Instead, a lot of reporting is formulaic, going through the motions and not presenting new ways of understanding problems. For example, there are many quantitative studies that test the validity of a framework such as TAM in the context of teacher use of technology. In these studies, the framework is introduced, the data are presented and a cursory explanation is given as to why TAM is useful or not in this context. The more interesting question as to why a TAM framework was used in the first place is neglected, it almost appears that the authors are hiding behind the theory rather than daring to create something original of their own.
- In a parallel criticism, there are a many small-scale qualitative studies which provide detailed description of a particular context but little theoretical

investigation. These can be engaging to read but do not draw out abstract concepts which would help the study connect to the wider world of social research.

- Researchers are technocentric in the way they think about technology and overestimate its impact. They are often excessively optimistic about technology too and have failed to produce a theory of organisational change to explain that optimism.

Are these criticisms fair? Before answering this question we need more to go on and Chapters 3, 4 and 5 assist by providing an overview of theorising, first, into technology and learning, next, teaching with technology, and, finally, the theorisation of technology itself.

Summary

In this chapter I have:

- explained that theory is a confusing concept as it carries different meanings;
- set out seven types of research into technology and education and discussed how each can make a theoretical contribution;
- shown that explanation is core to theory and identified different kinds of explanation in social research;
- suggested that theory has distinctive characteristics, it offers a particular kind of explanation which is more reliable, critical and transferable; and
- given space to theoretical shortcomings in relation to technology and education research alongside some strengths.

Where to read more

For more on theory and its different associations see both Abend (2008) and Krause (2016), who come up with broadly similar perspectives. I came across Sutton and Staw (1995) late in the day but this offers a very useful explanation of what theory is by setting out what it is not. They make the point too that social research does not need to be 'theoretical', but researchers should be self-aware and not claim to be making a theoretical contribution when they are not. Biesta et al (2014) take a more – can I say? – theoretical look at British and continental European ideas of theory, for example drawing attention to the roots of the word theory in the Greek idea of a *theatron*, the place from which spectators can see life played out in front of them. Attitudes to theory seems to shift not only across fields but by position in that field so that, as Evans (2002) suggests, practitioner researchers might feel they are making a contribution to practice in ways that more 'disciplinary' researchers might not understand.

I have categorised research output in terms of goals rather than methodologies and methods as there is very little written about the former and much written about the latter. Indeed, when it comes to research methods books there are many general books to choose from, including Punch (2009), Creswell and Creswell (2017) and Robson and McCartan (2016), all of which go into detail about the design of a project and weigh up the strengths and limitations of different methods.

There are many books too on particular types of analysis. Coolican (2019), for example, provides a guide to the role of the quantitative project in psychology and has a useful chapter on report writing. Miles et al (2013) is a particularly detailed practical guide to coding, representing and writing about data, as is Braun and Clarke (2019). Thomas (2016) is a good guide to case study, and notes the different purposes for carrying one out, the range of methods used as well as the depth of immersion in the case. A useful guide to survey research is Nardi (2018), which provides an overview of validity and reliability, issues in the collection of data and analysis of different kinds of data. If you want to take an explicitly statistical approach to modelling then there are many books to choose from. For example, Keith (2019) starts from bivariate regression (relationships between two variables), goes on to multiple regression (analysis of the influence of several variables on outcomes) and then to structural equation modelling (a term used to refer to a range of approaches which evaluate the fit between theoretical models and observed data). For more on meta-analysis, Higgins (2018) gives a good overview of its pros and cons and an introduction to statistical methods along the way. He sees meta-analyses as one contribution to the process of developing educational practice. For systematic review, at least for a purist approach, try Torgerson (2003). Learning analytics and Big Data are relatively new fields for education research and some applications and arguments are discussed in Williamson (2017).

In the qualitative tradition, Strauss and Corbin (1990) provide a grounded, or bottom-up, guide to coding, theorising and drawing conclusions from the data. They discuss the diagrammatic representation of findings, too. The publishing world is not short of introductory guides to action research (for example, McNiff, 2017) either, and most will assist you in carrying out a project.

If interested in typologies and learning styles in particular, there are many studies which categorise learners by their preference for Visual, Audio, Reading and Kinaesthetic (VARK) modes of learning (for example, Morze and Glazunova, 2014). VARK is often viewed very critically (see, for example, Hall and Moseley, 2005).

I began the chapter with a look at education as a distinctive field. Barnett (1994) makes an interesting case for a kind of 'real world knowing' that combines the insight provided by discipline theory with the concerns of practice. This implies that theory can be at the service of education if it is used to throw light on problems of teaching and learning, rather than, as in some other fields of social science, to address academic questions within a discipline. Hirst (1965) expressed a similar view much earlier, arguing that education needed to be guided by theory but not to be led by it.

Critiques of technology research are cited in the chapter and Selwyn (2011a) sees repeated over-optimism brought on by a neglect of social theory. It is easy to run away with the idea that education research is a poor relation when it comes to social science, but each field of research carries distinctive strengths and weaknesses. For example, discipline studies such as politics and sociology are often much more theoretically informed than practice fields such as education but a weakness of those fields is a tendency to follow whatever theory is in favour at a particular time (see, for example, reflections by Anderson, 2016).

2

What is theorising?

In Chapter 1 we saw that theory was a multi-faceted concept but carried within it a common idea: theory abstracted from the data in order to explain what was happening and why it was happening. Moreover, a theoretical explanation was expected to contribute to a discourse about technology and learning, and make justifiable, critically aware claims backed up with content knowledge and knowledge of research methodology. This was helpful, but I did not explain how researchers might go about the work of developing theory and, more specifically, how they might move from describing to explaining what they had found. This gap is addressed in this chapter, which looks at theorising. It is divided into three sections, which cover:

• Describing and explaining: how do they differ?
• Does theorising require another way of thinking?
• Is theorising making it up?

Describing and explaining: how do they differ?

What are researchers doing when they are theorising and how does theorising look different to other kinds of research reporting? To address these two questions I begin by focusing on the difference between *describing* and *explaining* set out in Chapter 1: describing is about what happened while explaining is about why it happened. Both are core to research output, and the differences between them can be subtle. For example, statisticians talk of *descriptive* statistics (in contrast to *inferential* statistics) not only when they categorise data but when they explain by drawing attention to associations between variables, say, in the form of scatter plots or statistical tests. Moreover, qualitative researchers differentiate between *thin* and *thick* description. Thin description describes actions as they appear on the surface, while thick description covers the meaning of actions and represents a theoretical contribution in its own right. For example, the discussion of routines in Olson (1988) might be thought of as an example of thick rather than thin description.

It seems then that categories are helpful in drawing attention to different kinds of reporting and the approach I take here is to differentiate between *basic*, *interpretative* and *analytical* description and between *narrow* and *wide* types of explanation (see Table 2.1). These categories are illustrated in the

Table 2.1: Typology of reporting, from description to theoretical explanation

Type of reporting	Typical features	Examples	Degree of abstraction from the data
Descriptive reporting			
Basic description	Charts, tables, numbers and percentages of responses, units. Numerical reporting of codes, giving quotes.	15 per cent of people were unable to access online resources. One person said 'the programme was difficult to use'. There were 25 occurrences of data coded as 'reticence' in the interviews. There were 256 messages sent to the forum in 2022.	Low
Interpretative description	The key take-aways within the data are identified. Any direct quotes are contextualised.	A key concern for most participants was the stability of the programmes. Students were asked to directly participate in live classes but most chose not to do so. Teachers' views of the IWB differed from those of the students in respect to ease of use.	Low/middle
Analytical description	The relationship between different findings or factors are drawn out, often in tables or models. Key ideas and concepts are used to integrate findings.	There was a significant correlation between age and gender when it came to take-up of computing as a subject in school. User reticence within forums was widespread and captured a reluctance to have ideas open for criticism.	Middle
Explanatory reporting			
Narrow explanation	Reasons for relationships within models or tables are given. Reasons for concepts and their consequences.	The explanation for the association between use of the programme and better learning outcomes lay in the personalised pathways for learners. The reason why girls were less likely to take up computing lay not so much in the subject but the way the subject was taught. They wanted a less formal and more problem-based approach.	Middle/high
Wide explanation	Evokes and assesses the suitability of concepts from the literature when explaining. Shows awareness of epistemological assumptions.	A theoretical backing for this model of learner engagement comes from the work on community of practice (for example, Lave and Wenger). In the light of these and other more recent findings gender and computing needs to re-theorised in more fluid and subtle ways. This model is not predictive rather it sensitises other researchers to key issues when developing online forums.	High

sections that follow, though note that the boundaries between each are fluid. Moreover, the move from one category to another, perhaps to one that is more abstract and analytical, is not necessarily sequential or indeed necessary.

Basic description

This covers simple statements, or tables, of what a researcher has found or what people have said: for example, '30 people were able to access Zoom for a live class, five could not'; 'Tutors talked for 60 per cent of class time, students for 15 per cent'; 'There were 52 questions asked, five answered without prompts, 32 with prompts and 15 not answered at all'; 'There were two cases of failed internet connections' and so on. Basic description, as far as feasible, provides an objective account of what happened though, of course, the researcher's judgement and interests come into play when considering which data are important to collect and how these data should be categorised (for example, the number of questions asked by a tutor might be a focus of interest in one study of live online classes but type of question much more relevant in another).

There are, of course, judgements to be made when it comes to categorising data, for example, when reporting on age groups is it better to have five- or ten-year groups, and should we have binary categories (high/low users of technology) or a more nuanced range? Even categories which at first sight appear objective require subjective judgement. For example, in our Zoom class an utterance might be classed as a question if there is an inversion of subject and verb, and use of auxiliaries such as *do* and *have*. However, questions are also signalled by rising intonation and teacher pausing, so what level of intonation, and what length of pause, makes a statement a question? And, in the same vein, what precisely constitutes internet failure in a live class – a total loss of connection or intermittent loss? These and other issues can of course be cleared up by being explicit when organising data, but even bare-bones descriptive reporting is not as straightforward as it appears.

For economical presentation much basic description is presented in tables and charts. For example, Table 2.2 contains part of a table showing the number of messages and words posted by participants (n=26) across the three weeks in which a class discussion forum was running.

The table presents the data clearly but a supporting text is nearly always added telling the reader what to look for. Here, it would be tedious in the extreme if the supporting text merely gave a line-by-line commentary such as 'Table 2.2 shows that participant A sent five messages in week one, four in week two and two in week 3 and produced a total of 440 words (excluding pasted text)'. Instead the researcher will, or should, draw attention to what is significant in respect to their research question. For example, in relation

Table 2.2: Number of posts and words during the active phase of the discussion

Participant	Number of posts				Total words
	Week 1	Week 2	Week 3	Total	
a	5	4	2	11	440
b	2	3	5	10	363
c	7	9	3	19	969
d	3	0	0	3	53
e	0	1	0	1	15
...					
x	6	5	2	13	525
y	1	3	7	11	279
z	2	11	1	14	1,450
Total N	79	120	68	267	13,629

to the question of who participated in this forum and to what degree, we might say that Table 2.2 shows:

> [p]articipation was uneven. On one hand, there were many messages (267) sent over the three-week period and some participants posted regularly and at some length. On the other hand, some participants did not post at all, or did not post in particular weeks, and over three-quarters of the messages were posted by a quarter of group members.

There is more to description than meets the eye. For example, Smahel et al (2020) offer a largely descriptive survey of how often children in 19 European countries used different technologies and their perceptions of 'media access, practices and skills, risks and opportunities, and social context'. The questionnaire appears to be framed with a theoretical model in mind, but the reporting is for the most part presented descriptively (and for that matter economically using diagrams and a supporting text which pulls out any findings of note). As an example, the survey confirms previous research that shows the use of smart phones to be widespread among young people and that favoured activities included accessing social networks and entertainment online. Data are broken down by country, age group and gender. There are differences in how girls and boys use technology but these are not as pronounced as often reported. There are also interesting contrasts between children in different countries which suggest directions for new comparative research. Why, for example, should children watch television more often in Spain than children in Italy? There is a note of realism too in talking about online safety. Researchers found, as expected, that many young people had had unpleasant experiences using the internet but also found that difficulties were often adequately dealt with by discussing with a friend or with family. Not all research activity needs to explain, description might be a quite justified goal in itself.

Interpretative description

By drawing attention to what is important in the data, the researcher is already starting on an *interpretative description* and there are many ways in which this can be further developed. For example, a study of online forums may have begun with an interest in the way that participants express themselves online. In fact, it is often suggested that online texts are less formal than other kinds of writing, but was this true in our study? To answer the question the researcher may break down messages according to 'register' (the particular variety of language used), exploring details such as sentence length, use of abbreviations and emojis, evidence for use or non-use of spell checkers, use of colloquialisms and so on. Alternatively, the researcher may be more interested in categorising the functions of messages rather than the way they are written. Messages might be broken down as *social* (for example, introducing each other or sharing news), *administrative* (for example, directions and discussions around assignment topics, organisation of work groups) or *cognitive* (for example, presenting and debating views on subject content). The underlying idea here might be that while not all messages need to have a cognitive focus, a significant proportion are needed if the forum could be described as a learning community, as opposed to a support community (see Table 2.3). Albeit just how many such messages there should be is open for debate.

Categories can be broken down further. For example the cognitive category might be subdivided between lower-order interactions (say, a request for clarification of an idea) and higher-order interactions (say, the stating of claims and provision of evidence in support of a claim). This is important as there would need to be a noticeable number of higher-order cognitive interactions for the forum to count as a space for academic argument.

Of course, none of this job of coding messages, or for that matter coding of interviews, observations and indeed literature, is straightforward, each

Table 2.3: Breakdown of messages according to function

Level	Frequency with which messages (n=277) were coded
Social	134
Administrative	67
Cognitive	76

step requires discussion and moderation with peers and experts and, where appropriate, 'member checking', that is, feedback from research participants. Whatever steps are taken to reduce subjectivity or bias are not foolproof, for example the much-promoted idea of inter-rater reliability might address eccentric coding choices but might end up only confirming that the two or more researchers taking part in such checks have a shared bias.

Analytical description

It is now a short step from interpretative description towards a more *analytical description* which attempts to show how categories, codes or themes work together. In a qualitative study, this might be done by introducing new concepts, or phenomena, and by exploring their consequences for the use of technology. For example, in Chapter 1 it was suggested that the concept of 'familiar routine' was important in understanding teacher attitudes to classroom technology and this helped explain the reluctance some teachers had for using computers (Olson, 1988). Perhaps in the case of forums, the concept of 'reticence' (a heightened awareness of the risk involved when presenting ideas to others, even in closed, moderated forums) may be a way of explaining some members' non-participation. Reticence might be associated with a fear of showing that you have not understood the subject matter, or worse pretending that you had and were now going to be found out, and might extend to a fear of being mocked if you have not followed online writing conventions. Digging deeper, reticence might be an individual characteristic but it might carry a contextual element. For example, you might be particularly reticent in asynchronous forums as in these it is difficult to gauge other people's reaction or 'take back' what you have said in the way you can do when talking in person. Reticence should then be taken seriously but perhaps it could be addressed through giving positive feedback and accepting the encouragement of others. Whatever, the case, reticence looks like a concept which might help us understand what is going on in the mind of the learner.

Furthermore, it might be possible in a larger quantitative study to develop analytical descriptions by looking at which particular groups of people are more reticent, for example, are females more reticent than males? Table 2.4 provides a breakdown of male/female students (in this study sample sizes for those that identified outside these two categories were too small for statistical testing) against reticent (those who participated rarely or not at all)/communicative students (those who participated more often). In fact, on simple inspection there does not seem to be a marked gender difference and a chi-squared test fails to show statistical significance at $p<0.05$ (The p-value is 0.216). If gender is not a 'significant' influence on level of participation, as might once have been expected, then this needs to be explained, say, by the particular context of the study (were steps taken to promote an inclusive learning culture?) or in terms of wider changes in gender identity and society

Table 2.4: Breakdown of reticent and communicative members by gender (n=177)

	Male	Female	Total
Reticent	35	41	76
Communicative	56	45	101
Total	91	86	177

(are there heightened expectations of inclusivity?). But, before giving up on the idea of gender as influential in discussion forums, researchers might want to look more carefully at the characteristics of the messages that men, women and non-binary people write. For example, in the past some researchers believed that women were more likely to produce 'person-centred' messages, characterised by using the names of the members to whom they were replying, and employing 'hedging' and other devices to signal empathy, but was this the case in your study?

Narrow explanation

Analytical description is already explanatory, but explanation in academic reporting tends to discuss relationships within the data in a more abstract way, often focused on the conceptual categories generated within a study. In many studies, the quest for explanation will lead to the production of diagrams and models. For example, Amichai–Hamburger et al (2016) carried out a review of papers on participation in online discussion and presented a 'typology of factors' that explained reasons why some members, disparagingly referred to as 'lurkers' in the literature, do not contribute. These factors are broken down by internal or psychological (individual difference), community (social group processes) and technology factors.

Figure 2.1 abstracts out what is important in 'lurker' behaviour and offers a hierarchy of concepts so that, for example, 'social loafing' is categorised as an aspect of wider social group processes. However, the diagram cannot stand alone and the supporting text provides a commentary that places the findings in the context of the literature. This allows Amichai–Hamburger et al (2016) to speculate how and why the relationships between variables occur. For example, non-participation may be a result of member social inhibition, an aspect of personality, which

> often prevents lurkers from posting online, leaving them to lurk in the background. In keeping with this viewpoint, Nonnecke and Preece (2001) suggest that lurkers display introverted behavior as they prefer to observe rather than contribute to discussions. Nearly a third of participants (28%) in Nonnecke and Preece's (2001) study stated that

Figure 2.1: Determinants of 'lurker' behaviour

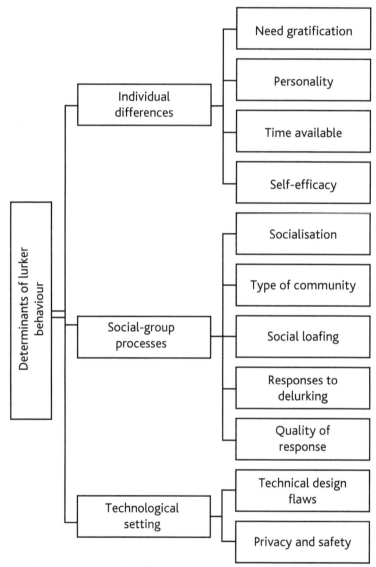

Source: Amichai-Hamburger et al (2016)

they were indeed shy about posting. From this perspective, it would seem that individuals who score highly on the introverted continuum tend to behave unresponsively in online groups. (Amichai-Hamburger et al, 2016: 270)

This explanation is needed as the authors' diagram is more a typology than a model, for it is not clear how the boxes are connected or why they should be. In fact, in any explanation it is a challenge to identify the direction of cause and effect as very often the lines or arrows that link factors or categories work both ways. For example, learning analytics researchers have spent a lot of time and effort in seeking to establish a relationship between level of online participation and learning outcomes (in particular assessment outcomes). When such a relationship does seem to exist it is, however, very difficult to say what is going on: are academically successful students more likely to post in the first place (perhaps they have greater academic confidence?) or are those posting in forums more likely to end up academically successful (perhaps they have gained from the experience of expressing their ideas?). On the face of it, both seem possible, but which should be prioritised?

The idea of breaking explanation down into narrow and wide categories is that some researchers stick very closely to the concepts developed within the field of education and technology research and some take in literature from cognate and discipline fields. A narrow focus can make a useful contribution in its own right, and some would argue that researchers have no right to go into more speculative areas. But there is value in casting the net wide. For example, a lot of writing about technology has drawn attention to its disruptive potential, that is, it can serve as a trigger for helping schools change to better fit the societies they serve. However, many of the contributions around disruption are 'narrow' and work within at times romanticised notions of technology (something I discuss in Chapter 6). A wider economic and social perspective can help us see that schools are not unique when it comes to resistance to change. A wider perspective might also lead to a more nuanced understanding of the consequences of disruption for it seems clear that while technology can throw relationships up in the air, asymmetries of power quickly re-establish themselves in new online environments. Moreover, there appears to be an enduring importance given over to routines and stability even in the face, or particularly in the face, of rapid social change (see, for example, Giddens, 1990).

Wide explanation

There is value then in *wide explanation*, and becoming more aware of the debates and concepts as discussed in other fields. Trying to achieve this wider outlook poses three key challenges: what to read; how to write about reading; and how far to go in reading about epistemology/ontology.

First, what to read. An initial challenge is that there is simply so much published and not enough time to read it. For example, if researching cooperation and collaboration there is a raft of empirical case studies and systematic reviews to consider covering both online and physical contexts. In particular, there is an earlier research tradition established by Johnson and Johnson (1989) and Johnson et al (1998), which has been very influential, though open to critique. There is, further, general learning theory dealing with language and intersubjectivity to take in (for example, work by Vygotsky and Dewey) as well as smaller ('middle range') theories such as 'positive interdependence' (that is, learners' perception that each group member plays a part in group success); social interdependence (that is, learners have to care about the group and come to derive self-identity from being a member of a group); theories of 'empowering' (that is, developing a belief in one's ability to make decisions and influence institutions); and the social contact hypothesis (that is, prejudice will break down on contact with others). This creates an almost impossible tension between wanting to explore the wider context and needing to home in on what is relevant for one's own particular study.

A second, and related challenge, when it comes to the literature is whether to be humble or critical when examining authoritative voices. On one hand, some researchers are unduly reverential and very circumspect in criticising a writer or deviating from what has become the accepted interpretation of a research tradition. This is understandable but can lead to hiding behind other writers rather than expressing your own views. One symptom of this reticence is to put your doubts about a theory down to a failure to understand it properly. This is doing yourself a disservice and it is worth remembering that certain writers become elevated because they capture a concern in the community at a particular point in time, but the basis on which they have generated their ideas might be quite weak. For example, when it came to learning theory, behaviourist theorists often drew conclusions on the basis of experiments conducted on animals, or conducted on humans in laboratory conditions, and the relevance of both for classroom research is questionable. In a different tradition, Piaget drew conclusions from small-scale experiments with his children and those of his colleagues; Vygotsky's writings seem to be based on recall of lectures and notes by others and there is considerable debate as to what he really did want to say. This is not to carp; these writers offered useful and imaginative concepts, but their ideas are there to re-work and re-interpret, they are not offering lasting truths about learning.

On the other hand, some researchers are by nature dismissive of the idea of authorities and want to develop their own models and concepts by themselves before becoming overly influenced by an imperfect research field.

This stance may be derived from a methodological position (for example, grounded theorists put off reviewing the literature until the end of a study as a point of principle) or it might come about via a critique of the ways in which previous research has been skewed to dominant interests as argued, say, in feminist and decolonising methodology. Moreover, there is stream of thinking about technology and education research which sees digital tools as shaping society so profoundly then whatever came before has little value. As I argue through the book there is a strong argument for critical questioning of the past but not for throwing away all previous insight.

A third challenge is that as researchers go wider then more and more they are drawn into questions of research methodology, including stances on epistemology and ontology which are so much a feature of social theory. Here, the perennial questions concern the degree to which our activity is shaped by social and material structures and to what degree we can exercise agency. For example, both Hamburger and Davis saw learner/user behaviour as very much determined by a series of factors, in a way that harks back to an earlier positivist tradition of social research. This helps in identifying the conditions in which decisions are made though, confusingly, some of the 'factors' operating on the individual are traits (for example, self-efficacy in Hamburger) or perceptions (for example, ease of use in Davis) which belong to the individual, making the individual both subject and object of an action. Anti-positivist approaches take a different tack and focus much more on agency as can be seen for example in action research projects cited in Chapter 1. This often has more appeal to education researchers as education itself is, after all, about promoting agency, however some practitioner accounts can end up romanticising both learning and technology.

Does theorising require another way of thinking?

It is comforting to see the shift from describing to explaining as a step-by-step process. This is certainly how it appears when researchers 'write up' their reports, but this is not, or at least not often, how it happens in practice. Indeed, if theorising is about the noticing of patterns within the data then why some patterns stand out and not others is something of a mystery. What does seem clear is that theorising requires commitment and passion and here well-used metaphors for the theoriser are that of a detective trying doggedly to solve a mystery, or a journalist willing to pursue leads without fear or favour. This is the picture presented by Swedberg (see, for example, Swedberg, 2012, 2016) who sees theorising as a rather obsessive process of discovery in which researchers draw on their personal ideas and experiences. For Swedberg, a different way of thinking is needed to theorise, one which is more intuitive, less procedural, than other steps in the research process. This is a kind of guesswork based on our capacity to make patterns out of observations, something which Swedberg (2012: 19–20) describes as 'abduction' – a term first used by the pragmatist philosopher Peirce (1839–1914) when recalling his investigation of the theft of his watch. Indeed, when talking to colleagues about their experiences of theorising, I found that many would describe their frustration when looking for insight and how they would go 'round in circles' before a kind of 'aha moment', when things fell into place (Hammond, 2018). Eventually they found unexpected links with ideas and concepts with which they were already familiar but had not hitherto seen the relevance of. Theorising is not about the justification of an idea but getting the idea in the first place. Once you have hit upon an idea that captures what is important in your study you can develop it by further reading and by checking the data once more. Indeed, what seemed a breakthrough might turn out to be a false trail, but an 'aha moment' is not to be ignored.

Theorising often feels serendipitous and difficult to explain, but nonetheless I will make the effort. Some time back I carried out my own doctorate research into online forums and was trying to make sense of my conflicting data on participation. I wanted to understand how and why some people took part in forums and some did not. The problem it seemed for many was lack of time. There was some literature to draw on but these were early days and as is often the case with technology a lot of studies were overly optimistic about participation and in a way that did not match some of the experiences of my interviewees. How to bring lack of time into my study?

I was thinking about this one evening as I was going to the theatre to see the play *As You Like It*. There was a 40-minute journey and I remember time passing quickly. I was not paying attention to the journey, I was still thinking about an interview I had carried out that day. When the play began, as often happens to me with a Shakespeare play, I started looking at my watch wondering how long this was going to last. But, in time, I became accustomed to the language and as I became absorbed the play raced by. However, I was pulled up in Act Three by the celebrated exchanged between Rosalind and Orlando in the forest of Arden (Shakespeare, 1598/1997: Act 3, scene 2). Did time pass at a constant pace?

Rosalind: By no means, sir: Time travels in divers paces with divers persons. I'll tell you who Time ambles withal, who Time trots withal, who Time gallops withal and who he stands still withal.

Orlando: I prithee, who doth he trot withal?

Rosalind: Marry, he trots hard with a young maid between the contract of her marriage and the day it is solemnized if the interim be but a se'nnight, Time's pace is so hard that it seems the length of seven year.

Orlando: Who ambles Time withal?

Rosalind: With a priest that lacks Latin and a rich man that
hath not the gout, for the one sleeps easily because
he cannot study, and the other lives merrily because
he feels no pain, the one lacking the burden of lean
and wasteful learning, the other knowing no burden
of heavy tedious penury; these Time ambles withal.

Orlando: Who doth he gallop withal?

Rosalind: With a thief to the gallows, for though he go as
softly as foot can fall, he thinks himself too soon there.

Orlando: Who stays it still withal?

Rosalind: With lawyers in the vacation, for they sleep between
term and term and then they perceive not how Time moves.

In other words, people experience time differently. Not a difficult concept but one expressed poetically in Shakespeare so that time *sleeps*, *gallops*, *ambles*, *trots* or *stands still*. The words resonated in a small way with my own experience of the evening: time passing quickly as I made my way to the theatre, then slowly as the play began and then more quickly again as I got into the play. I later read the scene at home and this triggered a memory of having seen the same text quoted in something I had read. With some searching I found that it was Hargreaves (2001: 100–101), who used the scene to introduce a section on the concept of 'phenomenological time' in reporting on teachers' lives. This felt deeply relevant to my study of online forums and perception of time became an organising principle for understanding my interview data: some of my interviewees could 'trot merrily' while others 'ambled' when it came to finding time to take part. This insight was not exactly earth-shattering but it did allow me to see my data in a different way and led on to a wider concern to understand the perspective of the learner. It was not the solution to a problem but the start of another way of thinking about participant behaviour.

What made this phenomenological framing such an important theoretical insight for me was the way it altered how I thought about my whole set of data rather than just a one-off interview. Again, in my work talking to colleagues, I found they too often talked about theorising as the emergence of a concept or idea that helped to integrate their diverse findings. Theorising represents a breakthrough; it was, in the words of one:

> to suddenly make sense of it. You read it in a different way. Your main focus at the beginning is on getting the key points but when you find a theory that works you are thinking not only do I understand this but this is really helping me to do this and useful ... rather than ... I am fighting against it. (Hammond, 2018: 5)

I have found few accounts of this process in social research but one researcher who wrote about integrating theory was the pioneering ecologist Rachel Carson (2018). She began in the late 1950s and early 1960s looking for what was common to a set of assorted facts about the environment: piles of dead songbirds here, the precipitous decline of eagle populations there, decimation of fish populations and so on. She concluded that they were the effects of indiscriminate spraying of toxic chemicals used to manage the land. As she put it:

> I have a comforting feeling that what I shall now be able to achieve is a synthesis of widely scattered facts, that have not heretofore been considered in relation to each other. It is now possible to build up, step by step, a really damning case against the use of these chemicals as they are now inflicted upon us. (Lear, 2009: 340)

This captures not only the way that an explanation integrates different sets of events, it also shows how theorising can uncover what afterwards seems blindingly obvious, but can only be achieved with a great deal of internal wrestling.

Theorising, then, is about reflecting, perhaps daydreaming about the research, and is difficult to legislate for. Talking of theories as leaps of the imagination or falling into place almost suggests that they come out of thin air, but they do not. We inherit a language that helps us make sense of what we observe and a set of concepts and ideas that inform our attempts at theorising. To theorise you have to be well-read but the request to theorise is often interpreted as advice to read more, and that is not always going to help. You may well have already read what you need; it is the application that is important. Cole and Engeström (1993: 1) express this well when they write: 'Everything has been thought of before; the task is to think of it again in ways that are appropriate to one's current circumstances.'

Is theorising making it up?

The picture I have given of theorising is that it is in important respects guesswork and this might sit uneasily with the image that some social researchers want to project about their trade. Paradoxically perhaps, natural scientists often embrace the speculative aspects of theorising in ways that some social scientists do not. Indeed, the way we think about scientific discovery was changed by Kuhn's idea of scientific paradigms (Kuhn, 2012/1962). Kuhn took on the widely held view that scientific knowledge was objective and cumulative. He argued that 'normal' science took place within dominant paradigms, ones that scientists were happy to accept as long as they could be used to find solutions to problems that mattered to them. But, at some point, a paradigm would fail to provide an explanation for new data, or for old data looked at in a new light, and a new theory was needed. A much-cited example is that astronomers worked productively within Ptolemy's view of the universe as a set of spheres surrounding the Earth, until this was turned on its head by Copernicus, who placed the sun at the centre of a system of orbiting planets. The history of science is characterised by these kinds of 'revolutions' or paradigm shifts. This suggests that we will never reach a complete view of how the world works; rather through our imaginative efforts we are forever producing good enough theories to get on with. The idea of science as creative enterprise, one that mixes leaps of the imagination with empirical testing, is often put forward by scientists themselves, most noticeably Einstein (see Howard and Giovanelli, 2019, for a summary), as well as other luminaries such as Medawar (1963) and Polanyi (1958), who started life as a natural scientist but then moved over to the philosophy of social science.

This more pragmatic view of science can lead to seeing the whole enterprise as 'ideological' (in the sense of pulling together the values and beliefs which provide coherence for a social group) rather than objective. However, most scientific theories end up being tested in controlled conditions, simulated or not, where their power to explain phenomena may be shown and provisionally accepted. Moreover, to the lay observer at least, the consequences of scientific discovery are demonstrable. There are good enough scientific theories for us to have gained incredible control over the natural world, so that under normal circumstances we can switch on an electric light, start a car, sit on a plane as it takes to the sky, converse via video link across thousands of miles and so on.

In contrast to natural science, social research creates theories which can and do influence policy makers and civil society, but their empirical application is always in doubt. This is because conditions are never as controllable as in *most* natural science, society is much more uncertain than experimental conditions can take account of. This means that, in our case, theories about technology in education are being generated and tested in very complex institutions (such as a school or college) and subject to the vagaries of teachers', learners' and policy makers' decision making. In addition, technology is fast changing so that what was once novel, and factored in as such, quickly becomes routine. To complicate matters, it is never clear whether being novel should count as a positive attribute, that is, as a particular tool is new it garners greater attention and interest, or negative, as it is new most people will struggle with learning to use it. The result is that the role of social research is more to inform, sensitise and suggest, rather than to provide a reliable prediction as to what will happen if you as a teacher or leader do X.

If we agree that theories are not tested in the same way in social research as they are in natural science, the question remains, 'Yes, but to what degree is social research value free and objective?'. This question takes us into an excursion around ontology and epistemology and those who stress the rigour, validity and generalisability of social research have often been described as 'positivist', committed to methods of natural science (or what they see as those methods) and to deductive logic in particular. Methodologically, deductive studies involve formulating quite specific hypotheses about phenomena, generally on the basis of reviewing what is known both practically and theoretically about a topic, and then testing them under experimental conditions (see Kang and Zhang, 2020; Hamilton et al, 2021 in Chapter 1 as examples). If the data support the hypothesis then the theory can be said to hold for that context – assuming that the research was well designed and carried out rigorously.

This 'hypothetico-deductive' approach is often associated with practical experimental research but it also underpins desk-based research such as large-N studies and systematic reviews. To make the approach work, researchers need to treat the concepts with which they are working as 'real', for example 'ease of use', 'engagement', 'motivation' or 'computer efficacy' can be satisfactorily defined, measured and their influence identified. They also need to assume that human behaviour can be explained, at least at the group level, by determining factors, a broadly behaviourist position, something I discuss in Chapter 3. Thus positivism, or our positivist legacy, leads to questions aimed at uncovering causality: 'What is the relationship between learning styles and online participation?'; 'What factors affect people's decisions to use a Massive Open Online Course (MOOC)?'; 'Does the use of online forums produce better learning?'. Positivists generally adopt a quasi-scientific language: tests are 'administered', 'validity' and 'reliability' are measured and they write in the third person. Positivists are more likely to speak confidently of a knowledge base.

Positivism can be, and is, attacked from many different directions but the most sustained critique came with the interpretivist shift in social research towards the end of the last century and into the present one. The interpretivist view stressed that studying humans is very different from studying natural phenomena as human beings exercise choice and learn to share, talk about and extend cultural practices together. In particular, symbolic acts such as making a sacrifice, showing respect, playing a game, only make sense if we can understand the rules and social practices which underlie them (Winch, 2007). In fact, we can add here that classrooms are richly symbolic and the performances of teachers and learners can be impenetrable without bringing background knowledge to what is going on – one reason why practitioner involvement in research is so important. Social research then requires very different methods and it is vital for the researcher to be able to 'step into the shoes' of social actors. Thus, interpretivism may ask questions such as: 'What do teachers see as the consequences of introducing a VLE into their schools?'; 'Why do people choose to use technology and others not?'; 'What kind of social capital do members create when they meet together online?'. In methodology interpretivists are more likely to undertake smaller scale case studies; adopt an exploratory approach to literature review; and use in-depth interview and other intensive methods of data collection. The language used by interpretivists will often reject the certainties of scientific discourse, researchers will 'explore contexts', 'engage with other viewpoints', 'negotiate understanding', rather than 'proving' or 'demonstrating'.

Positivist assumptions were slowly undermined over the previous century and the critique reached its height with 'postmodernism'. This was a loose term but was characterised by its scepticism around 'big ideas', the use of 'scientific methods', and the possibility, even the inevitability, of social and scientific progress. Postmodernism was critical of any notion of objective truth; in short, we believe what we choose to believe and what it is in our interests to believe and we create the most extraordinary claims for the objective and scientific basis for those beliefs. Going further, postmodernists seemed unwilling to accept scientific rationality as a privileged form of knowledge (Latour, 1999). Both natural and social science was in important ways 'making it up'.

It is easy to get the impression from this short account of research ontology (ideas of knowledge) and epistemology (how we access knowledge) that social research is dominated by paradigm wars, that is, a split between positivist and anti-positivist camps with no points of agreement. However, at least in my experience, this kind of mutual antipathy is rare among education researchers. In fact it is difficult to find anyone who self-identifies as positivist and if pushed those taking a deductive approach more often claim they deal in 'fuzzy generalisations', they are showing patterns of cause and effect that in all probability are worth looking at and may prove useful to inform, but not dictate, decisions about policy and practice (see Hasan, 2016). In contrast, those carrying out inductive studies will often talk about the relatability rather than the transferability of their work, but will claim, as much as anyone else, that the judgements they reach are defensible and supported by evidence. Going further, most education researchers today would see postmodernist thinking as a cul-de-sac, and new researchers today are far more interested in making a difference through their research than engaging in soul-searching about ontology.

Researchers' growing flexibility in respect to methodology and epistemology is one reason for the recent upsurge of interest in mixed methodology and pragmatism. In my view, it is helpful to simply accept objectivity as an unobtainable goal and reframe the enterprise of social research as a 'striving for truth'. This is not saying that 'anything goes', if we think that then we might as well give up on the whole idea of doing social research in the first place. Instead, we can work to reduce distortions by critical evaluation of *position* and *process* and hence create accounts which are credible and transparent, but never the last word.

In terms of position, we should, at an institutional level, question imbalances in how research communities are constituted (for example, is our community overly influenced by our obvious enjoyment of technology, by funding arrangements, or by gender and class) and, at a personal level, examine how our background and experiences affect our decision making. What was it, for example, that led me to see time as phenomenological? Of course, this was a subjective response but knowing that I was saying something that had been felt by others gave me the confidence to express my view.

As regards process, methods and practices need constantly to be held to account so that critical questions such as 'Are all relevant voices being considered when tackling a research problem?'; 'Are the procedures carried out as claimed?'; 'Are the claims justified?' need to be asked. This will in my case lead me to check and check again that at least some individuals in my study made statements that could be understood as recognising the subjective nature of time, and my interpretation of these statements could be checked with others, indeed with participants themselves. In theory, researchers should be able to say that any fair-minded reader could follow the steps taken in a study and see that their claims are justified, even if other claims are possible. In my case I would have had to establish that there was a chain of association between experience of time and online behaviour. Even if this association was inferred, the basis for the inference could be made clear. Finally, findings can be compared to work carried out by others to provide a greater degree of credibility (some would talk here about external validity). Replication should not, however, be forced, if there are reasons put forward why one case looks very different from others, then an explanation is strengthened not weakened. In my case, I could show how the concept of phenomenological time had a rich history in the arts and social research and draw attention to both the value of the concept and the difficulties that come with it.

Summary

In this chapter I have:

- shown the differences, often subtle ones, between describing and explaining;
- categorised explanations as narrow, contained within a set of data, or wider, drawing on a range of resources;

- explained how theoretical explanations require a different way of thinking; they are a mix of guesswork and desk work and
- explained how theories raise ontological uncertainty and suggested seeing research as a striving for truth.

Where to read more

My discussion of explanation and description is broad-brush and draws on my earlier discussion of academic writing (Hammond, 2022). My typology has some resonance with Bloom's influential taxonomy of learning. Bloom covered six major categories: Knowledge, Comprehension, Application, Analysis, Synthesis and Evaluation. A criticism of Bloom, or at least of those interpreting Bloom, has been a tendency to treat categories as discrete rather than fluid; this I have tried to avoid. There are other ways of exploring what makes a theoretical contribution, including Wilmot (2021) who offers an analysis of one student's writing on attitudes to climate change. This is much more fine-grained than I can offer here.

Swedberg (2012, 2016), already mentioned in the chapter, is both insightful and accessible when it comes to discussing theorising. Two older important inputs on theorising came from Eco (2015) and Mills (1959) – both were highly regarded academics interested in the process of research. Mills is very good on the importance of theoretical resources and the process of checking data against frameworks; Eco is worth reading not least for his account of 'misremembering' which shows that source material can be valuable even if misconstrued. There is not so much written about the experience of theorising but there is quite a lot on students' perspectives of carrying out a research project. Ylijoki (2001) identifies heroic, tragic, businesslike and penal stories of doing research, while Kiley (2015) explores different assumptions about theorising held by students from practice and academic backgrounds. Hjortshoj (2018) has a broader reach and looks at blockages on writing and support for the journey from 'student to scholar'.

The final section of the chapter touched on ideas of epistemology and ontology. Crotty (1998) remains a helpful guide to the philosophy of social research. There are a growing number of approaches that bridge the rather sterile positivism versus interpretivism divide. These include critical realism, crystallisation, mixed methods, pragmatism and post-positivism (see Hammond and Wellington, 2021).

Important criticisms of the deductive methods came from Mills (1959) and Glaser and Strauss (1967) and they remain thought-provoking today. Their critique of prevailing deductive social science at the time was that it left research a closed process in which researchers find only what they are primed to look for; researchers were being turned into technicians not theoreticians. However, Mills and Glaser and Strauss differed markedly in respect to literature. Reading and note-taking were very important to Mills, who wanted a historically and theoretically informed research practice; Glaser and Strauss were committed to a strongly inductive process in which literature was only consulted at the end.

If interested in the specific topic of coding posts in forums, go back to Henri (1992) for a first attempt at a typology; Gunawardena et al (1997) for an influential model; and Salmon et al (2010) for more on knowledge building. Work on gender and voice in online discussion has been influenced by Tannen (1991) – see, for example, Fauske and Wade (2003). I return to issues of both gender and decolonising methodology throughout the book. I also return to consideration of the wider economic social and economic context in theorising technology in Chapter 6. Fukuyama (2011) and Giddens (1990) are still interesting entries into debates about the nature of advanced capitalist societies.

As seen in the chapter, Cole and Engeström (1993) drew on Goethe's aphorism when reflecting on where theoretical ideas come from. This was expressed in the original German as 'Alles Gescheite ist schon gedacht worden, man muß nur versuchen, es noch einmal zu denken' (Goethe, 2016: 53). The idea, though this is a question of interpretation, is that we use intelligent ideas from the past to understand the present. This is very different from the idea that it has all been thought of before so there is nothing new to say.

3

Theorising learning with technology

Chapter 2 established the importance of drawing on what has gone on before when theorising. The following four chapters help us do this by delving into the debates around the use of technology in the past and how these debates are being framed in the present. The examples I give are not, of course, comprehensive but they set out ways in which arguments have developed. An obvious place to start is looking at theories of learning themselves. So much discussion of digital technology is about its contribution to learning, so how, if at all, do researchers use learning theory? In this chapter, then, we look at:

• Behaviourist theories (the mind as a closed box)
• Cognitivism (and the learner as meaning maker)
• Social constructivism (and the inheritance of tools)
• Community of practice and related theories
• Do we need learning theories?
• Theories specific to technology mediation
• Do we need theory in an age of Big Data?

Behaviourist theories (the mind as a closed box)

When computers were being introduced into education, back in the 1980s, there were, among all the excitement about modelling and exploratory programmes, repeated worries that digital technology, far from heralding a move towards more learner-centred approaches, would presage a return to drill and practice programmes, and 'a giant step backwards into the nineteenth century' (Chandler, 1983: 1). This raises the question as to what is so wrong with drill and practice?

The theoretical justification for drill and practice is based on behaviourist principles: desirable behaviour (such as learning a new topic) is the result of positive reinforcement of correct responses (at its simplest automatically generated feedback of *well done, congratulations, now let's go for another one*) and negative feedback or correction of errors and mistakes (Skinner, 1953). While behaviourist learning principles have been largely seen as suspect by educationalists (more on this in Johannesen and Habib, 2010, in Chapter 4), they have never gone completely out of favour. In fact, they are revisited in more recent times in popular software. For example, online behaviour reinforcement programmes such as ClassDojo reward young children with points for being on task, being helpful, completing assignments and so on; these points are stored and students are given rewards. Duolingo, the well-known language learning app, rewards students for successful recall as well. It offers old-style language learning, drills of decontextualised vocabulary and grammar structures, with dashboards showing progress, points for successful completion and suggestions for adaptive paths through the material.

The attraction of behaviourist learning theory is its intuitive appeal – we improve by getting feedback on performance – with its more subtle supporters saying it is positive feedback that makes the difference, not getting 'told off' when we get it wrong. Whatever we are learning we should practise and practise until we get it consistently right. As a theory of learning it is uncomplicated and appears credible. Behaviourists ask few questions about how the mind works: there is something going on in our heads, of course there is, but we cannot see what it is and there is no point in asking too many questions about it. Let us just concentrate on the association between behaviour and performance (see Figure 3.1). To its critics, however, what goes on in the mind is important and they point out that behaviourism is failing as a theory as it does not explain why some things which have been successfully 'learnt' through repeated practise are later forgotten or applied mistakenly. Neither does behaviourism explain how or why learners construct rules and are then able to apply them in new contexts. For example, in language learning how is a child able to form past tenses of verbs they have never come across before, or in mathematics how does a child who has learnt the two-, three- and four-times tables then recite the five times off their own bat? At its best, then, behaviourism seems to work if we are looking at simple recall of information rather than how the learner makes sense of rules or handles complex information.

In looking to offer an alternative view of learning theory researchers wanted to explore what was ignored, or glossed over, in behaviourism, in other words to provide an account as to how the mind worked. Here they drew on ideas of cognitivism, constructionism/constructivism and community of practice to provide metaphors for understanding.

Cognitivism (and the learner as meaning maker)

Cognitivist theory sees the learner as an active participant in learning – someone trying to make sense of new information on the basis of past

Figure 3.1: Behaviourist model of learning with the mind (shaded) as a closed box

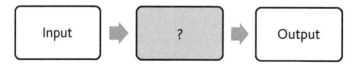

Figure 3.2: Cognitivist approaches with the mind (shaded) as an organiser of input

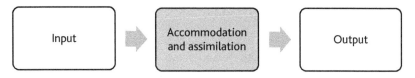

experience (see Figure 3.2). In cognitive approaches the learner is a meaning maker and here the three key terms are *schema, assimilation* and *accommodation*. Schema are the ways we have for organising our knowledge of a field, in other words we organise what we have experienced into patterns and systems, our minds are not full of unrelated facts. Assimilation occurs when incorporating new facts into existing schema. This may involve minor modification of the schema and/or re-interpreting the facts to fit the schema. Accommodation occurs when we recognise problems with an existing schema and, with the help of more knowledgeable others, we restructure our schema accordingly. Assimilation represents a more incremental kind of learning, accommodation a step change in understanding.

The value of the cognitive approach is that it helps us understand the complexity of learning new things. While assimilation and accommodation may be imperfect metaphors for how the mind works they are very useful concepts when it comes to diagnosing student development. For example, a student might believe as they go into a physics class that mass is the sole factor when it comes to the buoyancy of an object, that is, heavier objects will sink and lighter objects will float. They might then interpret any new experimental data through this misplaced organising principle even in the face of countervailing examples (see Driver, 2008). A teacher has to address this misconception head-on by giving a scientific account of buoyancy at an appropriate level (for example, 'although we think that heavier objects sink and lighter objects float, the key factor is the mass of the object relative to its volume. This means that ships can float even if they are heavy as long as their volume is sufficiently large'). Understanding conceptions and misconceptions is very important both for classroom teaching but also for designing online instructional material. Such material should not simply provide learners with practice but offer clear explanatory content which addresses the likely misconceptions of the learner (see Laurillard, 1993: 181–209). Better if this is done is a lively and interactive manner.

Cognitive theory is strongly associated with Piaget who was very concerned in exploring the developmental processes of the child over time. While Piaget's work is now critiqued for being overly rigid when it comes to what a child can learn at different ages, it has informed research into many contexts including learners' understanding of computer programming.

For example, Teague et al (2015) explained students' understanding of programming across three stages of development:

- A *sensorimotor* stage: here knowledge is 'fragile', learners have weakly developed ideas about programming and find it difficult to trace (or follow) code let alone understand underlying principles or write their own code.
- A *preoperational* stage: learners are beginning to master the semantics of code (for example, what different statements do) and can accurately trace code. However, they are not able to reason about the semantics of the program other than by inductive reasoning, that is, input of X results in Y.
- A *concrete operational* stage: students can reason deductively about a programming language and write non-trivial code.

The authors find these stages useful in assessing the development of learners' thinking and in considering the kind of input that will help them develop their programming competence. As practitioners, as well as researchers, Teague et al have an obvious interest in the shift from a lower to a higher level of understanding and see the learner journey as a series of overlapping and inconsistent steps, rather than discrete stages which once passed are never returned to. Thus learning is complex, at times unpredictable, but it is possible to categorise levels of understanding and consider how to provide students with the guidance and activities that will best support them.

A cognitive approach gives us useful insight into learning, but it is not without its shortcomings. In particular, at least in its classic formulation, it can be over-focused on what individual learners are doing or thinking, rather than the world of support around them. In fact this wider world of support becomes more and more important within networked societies. Computing is an interesting case here. Novice programmers can constantly experiment with a program for themselves and thus programming seems a suitable context for an independent or individualised learning approach. However, programming could, and arguably should, be taught in a more collaborative way so that learners can learn from each other. This would be more akin to the process of real-life programming work (for example, Nerland and Jensen, 2010) and indeed it is an approach that Clegg and Trayhurn (2000) and others advocate to address the gender imbalance in the take-up of computing.

Social constructivism (and the inheritance of tools)

In the search for a more holistic view of learning, researchers drew increasingly on principles of social constructivism. Here Vygotsky is a key figure, someone whose status in the education research community shifted from unknown Russian social scientist, active in the first two decades following the October 1919 revolution, to an icon of learning theory. Indeed, a search of Web of Science revealed that until 1990 there were no references to Vygotsky in abstracts of peer-reviewed articles but between 1990 and 1999 there were 232; 289 between 2000 and 2009; and between 2010 and 2019 there were 532. Of course this rise in part reflects the increase in the volume of articles produced in the social sciences, but it also shows how social constructivist principles influenced researchers in the later years of the 20th century and into the 21st century.

As with any tradition there is no universal agreement on key terms associated with social constructivism. There is also an understandable confusion between constructionism in the context of social theory and constructivism in respect to learning theory. In sociology, social *constructionism* focused on the perspectives that social actors have on their world and their search for meaning through their interaction in society. As a theory it is concerned not only with direct interaction but how interaction is shaped by social identity, for example, cultural assumptions around racial and gender identities that we inherit as members of society. Constructionists became increasingly interested in how interactions became routinised with Berger and Luckmann (1966) using the term 'reification' to describe the way that institutional arrangements are perceived as natural and timeless, rather than as products of agreements between human beings. In contrast, in learning theory social *constructivism* has a more particular interest in how the learner crosses a 'zone of proximal development': this zone being the difference between what the learner knows now and what they are capable of learning with the help of a knowledgeable other (Wood, 1988). Vygotsky and Cole (1978) see this as a move from one state of understanding to another, one which is more 'scientific' and provides a better match with subject knowledge in a particular field of inquiry. Vygotsky was particularly interested in the 'tools' which assisted learning, and these tools included material artefacts as well as cultural objects which are passed on to us, such as signs, symbols and language in its broadest sense. These tools mediate between subject (the learner) and object (what is to be learnt), as expressed in Figure 3.3.

All of Vygotsky's work is open to interpretation not least as so much seems to have been reconstructed from notes in translation (Miller, 2011). One important tension lies in whether Vygotsky believed he was offering a theory of instruction, that is, how to support learners to gain mastery of scientific terms and concepts in new ways, or whether he was more focused on the ways that learners could work together to create new knowledge using whatever resources were to hand. This has meant that social constructivism

Figure 3.3: Activity is mediated by tools

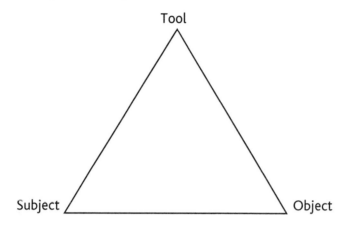

has been evoked to justify a range of practices from interactive whole class teaching to unstructured communities of practice.

Whatever Vygotsky's intentions, social constructivism, with its focus on tools, language and interaction, fits very well with computer-supported contexts. In one example, Nikolaidou (2012) looked at the collaborative interactions that emerged during computer-based music composition with pairs of 11-year-old pupils composing short melodies at the computer. In this study the computer was seen as supporting pupils as it enabled them to play back what they had composed and so to improve by discussing it with others and editing it. In the author's words the computer offered 'iteration and provisionality', that is, the opportunity to easily access and amend a product. However, Nikolaidou was also interested in pupils' talk around the computer and introduced a typology containing disputational, cumulative, exploratory, operational and reflective categories of peer talk. From this, she was able to propose a model for understanding talk and collaborative interaction and provide a 'better understanding of the nature of computer-supported collaborative creativity in primary music education'.

This kind of research enables us to reflect on the quality of the interaction around the computer rather than reach for the simplistic idea that talk in general should be promoted as it supports learning. The research also allows for a more fine-grained discussion of what technology offers (here provisionality and iteration) rather than a general statement of technological affordances. However, a criticism of this social constructivist tradition of research is that it is focused on the micro level of the classroom, and indeed only on particular aspects of student activity within the classroom, without looking at the school as a system or indeed what students do when not in school.

Community of practice and related theories

Through the influence of social constructivism, researchers became more and more interested in the social context of learning; learning became seen more as a joint rather than a personal undertaking. This shift towards the social reached its zenith with theories of communities of practice (CoP). Key figures here were Lave and Wenger (for example, Lave, 1977; Lave and Wenger, 1991; Wenger, 1998). Wenger (1998), for example, began by offering a critique of traditional, instructional teaching; learners were separated from the world outside the classroom and were expected to acquire discrete items of knowledge through their own efforts. Collaboration, at least when it came to assessment, was considered cheating. As a result, learning in institutions was seen as 'irrelevant, boring and arduous'. Faced with this situation, Wenger asked:

> [W]hat if we adopted a different perspective, one that placed learning in the context of our lived experience of participation in the world? What if we assumed that learning is as much a part of human nature as eating or sleeping, that it is both life sustaining and inevitable, and that given a chance we are quite good at it? And what if, in addition we assumed that learning is in its essence a fundamentally social phenomenon reflecting our own deeply social nature as human beings capable of knowing? What kind of understanding would such a perspective yield on how learning takes place and on what is required to support it? (Wenger, 1998: 3)

In introducing the idea of CoPs, Wenger explained that we took part in many different types of community, depending on where we lived, worked, how we spent our leisure time and so on. However, CoP were not there by default; these were communities in which we played a more active role, something which involved negotiating meaning with others. A CoP was then a joint enterprise even if not all members were equal in terms of level of participation and influence.

Communities had a history. As they evolved over time they had to establish rules and expectations around their scope and ways of working. The process of reaching agreement was described, borrowing a word introduced earlier in the context of social constructionism, as 'reification'. Of course, members could not turn a CoP into whatever they wanted; they were constrained by the context in which they were created. However, Wenger felt that members had opportunities to set out their own goals and interests as well.

So far Wenger's seems to be saying that communities support their members and achieve joint goals but this does not seem very far-reaching.

However, his really radical take on CoP concerned participation itself; participation in community should not be seen as a support for instrumental goals ('through interaction with others we will learn better'), but rather it was an end in itself ('participation in itself is learning'). This required a major rethink of the purpose of education away from products and outcomes and towards processes and patterns of interaction. It was, then, no surprise that CoP became an obvious point of reference for those researching online social networks once they became core to social and professional life. Examples, and there are a huge number on which to draw, include Inel Ekici (2018), who explored new teachers' sense of efficacy though participation in online professional communities; Mavri et al (2020), who looked at the benefits of online links between design students and industry professionals; and Hennckam et al (2020), who looked at how women composers supported each other's early careers within an online community.

Through the idea of CoP and related theories, researchers' focus shifted from computer as content provider, to computer as a tool for allowing support, collaboration and construction of new knowledge in online or hybrid groups. One consequence was that researchers increasingly looked beyond the classroom and became more and more interested in informal, or at least out-of-school activities, such as participation in online games, fan fiction, vlogging communities and so on (for example, Williamson et al, 2005; Gee, 2018). Indeed, young people's lives in and out of school were diverging more and more, at least when it came to their digital practice. Livingstone and Sefton-Green (2016) illustrate this in telling a story of a class of young learners in a London school and a teacher who rather tentatively wanted to set up a Facebook page to support an extra-curricular challenge the students were invited to take part in. The school carefully considered the associated risks and benefits of creating such a page in ignorance of the fact that the students had already done it. It is a story that can be repeated over and over.

The benefits of taking a CoP, or similar, approach are considerable: CoP expands our idea of what learning is; it celebrates or at least allows us to celebrate learner agency; it emphasises the importance of cooperation and sharing; it provides a good fit with a world dominated by social networks; it helps us notice informal or out-of-classroom learning. However, there are, of course, difficulties and objections.

First, is the assumption in, at least CoP itself, that formal learning is boring. We can all think of cases in which that is true, but is it really a general finding that learners are turned off classroom learning to the extent that Wenger had argued? Learners in many cases seem to like the routine of going to a physical classroom and rate teachers with good subject knowledge and pedagogic skills very highly even if their approach is direct and instructional. This can lead to the ironic situation that academics, who choose to spend their working lives in classrooms, are often more enthused by out-of-classroom learning than are students themselves. There is, as we discuss later, a clear role for the teacher, or at least for 'teaching presence'.

Second, learners can collaborate and achieve new knowledge about a topic but what is the status of the new knowledge gained? Could members of communities end up agreeing to things which were not thought through or indeed were outright irrational? In CoP the idea of reification tends to gloss over the quality of decision making and the ways that groups are constrained by imbalances in power by virtue of who members are rather than the quality of their contributions. We badly need a way of differentiating democratic and educational communities of practice from, say, hate groups, conspiracy theorists and, less perniciously, fan groups. Communities can be easily over-romanticised and the first wave of enthusiasm for open online communities became dimmed by the realisation that they can be a source of commodification, and worse a support for misinformation and discriminatory practices.

Third, why set up a barrier between what we learn as part of a community and what we learn as an individual? The two can be complementary and indeed if we take the example of teachers we would want them to be well-connected to funds of knowledge but we would still expect them to *possess* content and pedagogical knowledge in their own person. Salomon (1993) indeed argues that there are many occasions in which cognition is not distributed, for example academics might be well ensconced within distributed communities but at some point they will want to write alone and just get on with it by themselves.

Do we need learning theories?

Learning theory has value as it allows us to focus on particular aspects of teaching and learning and provide us with the concepts and vocabulary to describe what we see online or in the classroom. Moreover, learning theories provide powerful metaphors to think about learning: the mind as an empty box in behaviourism; the learner as restless meaning maker in cognitivism; an inheritor of a cultural achievements in social constructivism; member of a kind of learning club in CoP. Theories are practical too. Specific research questions, 'What kind of feedback is more effective?'; 'What is the value of shared talked?'; 'How do learners move towards a better understanding of physics?' can all be explored through the lens of learning theory.

For theories to remain useful they need to evolve as conditions change and as the questions researchers ask change. This has happened. The background to behaviourist theory was mass industrialisation and so-called scientific organisation of production in the earlier years of the previous century (Taylor, 1911); researchers wanted to ask questions about inputs and outputs as these mattered in 'scientific' systems. As the century wore on, researchers wanted to ask more questions about what the learner was thinking as there was greater discussion of the skills needed to manage in complex society, in particular skills such as learning to learn, adapting to change, exercising judgements and working with others (for example, Fullan and Langworthy, 2013). Not surprisingly this led to an interest in theories which focused on co-operation and community. Ideologically too, there was, post-1945, increasing importance given in some societies to promoting less hierarchical education systems, ones that might provide a rehearsal for participation in democratic society; behaviourism fell out of fashion and social psychology came in. This suggests that there are values at stake when it comes to theory and it is not surprising that many education researchers gravitate towards theories of social constructivism and cognitivism as these better reflect their concern as educators for developing learner agency.

Of course, theories cannot and are not designed to capture everything, that is impossible; all come with cracks and shortcomings (see Table 3.1). For example, a behaviourist might be impressed by, and focused on, the way a program provides students with carefully structured input and feedback at regular intervals, unaware that important learning has gone on within the online groups that students have set up and in which they share knowledge and ideas. In contrast, a researcher influenced by CoP theory might miss that there are learners who struggle to take an active part in group activity for both personal and contextual reasons. We should avoid being reverential about theories of learning and about theorists – no matter how impressed we might be at their ability to put into words things which we felt but had not been able to express for ourselves. Better instead to say we are working in a tradition proposed by Skinner, Vygotsky or Lave and Wenger, rather than saying we *are* behaviourist, social constructivist, or CoP researchers.

Theories specific to technology mediation

Theorists provide foundational ways of understanding learning and their theories can be applied to a range of settings. In fact each of the 'big' learning theories already discussed emerged out of research carried out in largely physical settings and were only later adapted to online contexts. Does this suggest we should we look for something that is more rooted in research with digital tools? We could try, and there are several approaches which seek to theorise co-participation online. These include ideas of distributed learning; networked learning; community of inquiry; knowledge building; and affinity spaces, to name a few. They are described briefly in what follows while connectionism, which became a popular alternative to CoP, is presented as my first boxed example (Case 3.1).

Table 3.1: Learning theories compared

Learning theory	Key idea	Implications for teaching and learning with digital tools	Strengths	Shortcomings
Behaviourism	Operant conditioning, reinforcement of correct responses	Promotion of drill and practice software using adaptable software	Provides explanations which are intuitive for some; focuses on measurable outcomes	Ignores what goes on inside our heads when learning
Cognitivism	Learners are meaning makers, information needs to be processed	Sensitivity to the different ways in which the learner experiences technology; consideration of misconceptions in software design	Curious about the process of learning	Focuses on the individual learner rather than the system
Social constructivism	Learning is social in that it involves artefacts, language and other people	Provision of models for organising both instruction and group work	Focuses on language and social tools	Can be too focused on micro-level interaction
Community of practice	Learning is participation	Promotion of social networks; awareness of the value of informal learning	Suited to the rise of online networks	Is overly optimistic about ways in which networks operate and the status of 'new knowledge'

The starting point for many in theorising learning mediated by technology is, as it is with Lave and Wenger, to think about learning as distributed in groups. For example, Perkins (1993) offered not so much a theory of learning but set out to consider how learning had become 'distributed' with the advent of computer networks. He noted that learning was not an individual undertaking. For example, in professional settings teamwork and wider collaboration was the norm; engineers did not design using 'what is in their head', but participated in networks in which they accessed resources and processed the views and inputs of others. Indeed, professionals need to possess *knowledge*, or a 'rich technical repertoire', but in important ways they relied on *retrieval* of past knowledge, they used tools to *represent* that knowledge in new situations and ultimately they *constructed* new original products. Work was everywhere mediated by information systems. This mattered a great deal for if we carried on thinking about learning as an individual undertaking we would not be preparing young people properly. As Perkins put it:

> active thinkers assemble around themselves a rich surround and interact with it in subtle ways to achieve results that would be difficult with the person-solo. They rely on the 'fingertip effect' assumption, presuming that people will automatically take effective advantage of the surround just because it is there. They thereby miss the opportunity to cultivate all sorts of skills, concerning the artful distribution of thinking and learning. (Perkins, 1993: 105)

Researchers have gone to elaborate on the idea of learning as distributed using concepts such as *computer supported cooperative learning* (CSCL) (for example, Stahl et al, 2006) and *asynchronous learning networks* (ALN) (see Wieland, 2012). Both traditions are interested in ways in which learners communicate with each other across a distance, albeit CSCL grew first out of an interest in synchronous communication and conversation analysis and ALN, as the name suggests, in the context of asynchronous virtual learning, online forums in particular. Both ALN and CSCL were rather niche and a broader concept was that of *networked learning* (NL), defined as a range of approaches to promote collaborative and co-operative connections in ways that were 'important to them (*learners*), and over which they had significant control' (see Jones, 2015; emphasis added). This led to a consideration not only of learner–learner interactions, but also learner–teacher and learner–resources interactions.

NL was not in itself a theory of learning, or at least not a 'grand theory', rather it was informed by different traditions of social learning theory to develop online pedagogy. It was concerned with developments in higher education but shared much with the idea of *connected learning*, more associated with the school sector. Again, connected learning was not so much a distinct theory but drew on social cultural learning theory to recognise the importance of 'connections across space and time'. A key interest for researchers was the connection (or they would say the lack of connection in present arrangements) between home, community and school learning, and the search for a pedagogy that would help young people makes sense of the world as it is today (see, for example, Kumpulainen and Sefton-Green, 2014).

In looking for a way of structuring online learning, *Community of Inquiry* (CoI) models were particularly helpful (see Garrison et al, 2001). CoI was inspired by a reading of Dewey and was characterised by four stages. First, the posing of a *trigger* question or event (set by a teacher or group member). Second, the *exploration* of solutions to this problem in both private and shared worlds involving, say, brainstorming, questioning and exchange of information. Third, the *integration* of, or the constructing of meaning from, the ideas generated in the exploring phase. This, it was suggested, required an active teaching presence to 'diagnose misconceptions, to provide probing questions, comments, and additional information in an effort to ensure continuing cognitive development, and to model the critical thinking process' (Garrison et al, 2001: 10). Fourth, the *resolution* of the problem by means of direct action by professional groups and more conceptual testing in academic contexts. A further aspect of the CoI model is the attention given to three different types of presence: teaching presence; social presence; and cognitive presence, all of which are important for learning to occur. CoI has much to offer as it presents a coherent teaching methodology but it has drawn some criticism. For example, Xin (2012) found it difficult to model in practice and argued for a more fine-grained approach to categorising presence.

A more radical understanding of online collaboration than I have considered so far is offered in knowledge building (KB) theory. This was set out and in a great many papers by Scardamalia and colleagues (for example, Scardamalia and Bereiter, 2006; Zhang et al, 2009) and discussed by Chan and van Aalst (2018) among others. KB began, like much other work discussed in this section, by addressing the need to educate young people for the 'knowledge age'. Again, like other theories, it noted that using new communication and content tools groups of learners (and they were interested in school students) were able to address shared problems and create their own knowledge. Scardamalia and Bereiter (2003) argued that learners should not be awed by what has gone on before but learn to assess its usefulness for 'the deliberate creation and improvement of knowledge that has value for a community'. One of the most important elements of KB was that of idea improvement, that is, willingness to work on the understanding of problems through inquiry. KB theory was optimistic that through joint problem solving and guided communication students could experience being authentic members of a KB community. This meant that students' participation needed to be evaluated according to their engagement with the process of KB rather than their 'conformity to accepted knowledge'. As argued by Goldman and Scardamalia, KB requires that students 'not only recognize that their own ideas, like ideas in general, are improvable, but see their work as part of a community process in which their focus in not simply on their own ideas but on the ideas of their community as a whole' (2013: 262).

The process of KB needed supporting for, while generating ideas appeared to come naturally to people, especially children, the sustained effort to improve ideas did not. KB, then, was distinctive for its interest in the idea of knowledge as provisional, and there to be critiqued, though critics wondered if its focus on processes over content left the coverage of subject knowledge as rather haphazard.

A final contribution to online learning considered here comes from the idea of affinity spaces (for example, Gee, 2005, 2018), which was offered as an explicit alternative to CoP theory. Gee defined two key concepts: *social semiotic spaces* (SSS) and *affinity spaces*. They were not synonymous. SSS was a general term to describe a space with an 'internal grammar' (its design) and an 'external grammar' (the organising of people around the space). Two further features of an SSS were the 'generator' – this triggered exploration and transformation of spaces – and 'portal' – something used to provide access in the first place. SSS was a neutral term (and could apply to both online and F2F spaces) but, drawing on his studies of computer-based gamers, Gee listed a number of features which defined an affinity space as a special kind of SSS.

It is a long list, but in brief Gee (2005) saw young people as flexible in their online participation and noticed an affinity between members rather than strong bonds. This meant that new artefacts or new knowledge created within an affinity space could be seen as owned by an individual as much as by the group. Affinity spaces worked as they were open and participants related to each other primarily in terms of 'common interests, endeavours, goals or practices', rather than social categories of age, gender or class, and it also meant that 'newbies and masters' shared a common space though they might participate in different ways. There were varied routes to leadership within an affinity space but any esteem earnt had to be based on demonstrable knowledge. Members exercised control over their participation.

For Gee, the key point about affinity spaces was that they looked nothing like the school classroom. To heighten the comparison, Gee notes that portals within an affinity space were themselves strong generators. For example, gamers may 'create new maps, new scenarios for the single-player and multiplayer games, adjust or redesign the technical aspects of the game, create new artwork and even give tutorials on mythology as it exists in the game or outside the game world' (Gee, 2005: 221). In contrast, classroom textbooks were very weak generators.

Criticism of affinity spaces often focus on the quality and extent of participation. For example in many online spaces, fan fiction and Scratch programming are examples, creators have vastly different levels of engagement and the work inside the space tends to be driven by relatively few participants. Others only contribute at irregular intervals and any feedback they give is superficial rather than what is needed to be able to push learning in the group along (see Magnifico et al, 2018).

A common thread in all the approaches discussed here is that they are drawing on past theory rather than proposing a new theory from scratch, as was the case with Siemens and connectivism (see Case 3.1). In most cases, they have developed over time but the fundamental ideas have been fairly consistent. Each takes an optimistic stance on collaboration and in different ways these theories are exploring what level of direction is needed to steer participation in suitable directions. Those struggling with these approaches will, as with CoP, question the quality of collaboration and the status of knowledge produced in groups.

Case 3.1: Connectivism, a learning theory for the digital age (Siemens, 2005)

What is this about?

This is a contribution to how we should think about learning theory in an information age. It is a critical exploration of past theory and does not present new data with a new set of interpretations, though other work by Siemens and Downes does this.

What is the key argument?

The key argument is that previous theory is outdated as it was not developed at a time when learning had been impacted by technology. Thus learning theory needs to reflect the way the world, and our learning about the world, has changed. These changes have included increased attention to knowledge management; awareness of the importance of regular updating of knowledge; and a shift to informal learning as a significant aspect of our learning experience. More startlingly, our constant exposure to computers has meant that the way we learn has changed: 'technology is altering (rewiring) our brains'.

Past learning theory does not address the role of digital tools as it is for the most part concerned with what is occurring inside a person's mind. For Siemens, even social constructivist theory focuses on the individual and does not properly address what is stored and manipulated by technology. Further, past learning theories have been concerned with the 'actual process of learning, not with the value of what is being learned'. In a networked world, we need to focus on the ability (or meta skill) of making sense of information: 'When knowledge is abundant, the rapid evaluation of knowledge is important.' Thus a completely new approach is needed.

What alternative does Siemens put forward?

He puts forward a different approach to learning, that of connectivism, which at its centre sees learning as making connections within digital environments. We cannot capture all the knowledge which is out there instead 'we derive our competence from forming connections'. Siemens sees learning as 'chaotic' in the sense that the challenge is to access many different networks but to 'recognize the patterns which appear to be hidden'. Siemens describes a network 'as connections between entities. Computer networks, power grids, and social networks all function on the simple principle that people, groups, systems, nodes, entities can be connected to create an integrated whole. Alterations within the network have ripple effects on the whole'. For Siemens this abundance of nodes provides a free market of ideas and he suggests there will be a 'gravitational pull' so that nodes that 'specialize and gain recognition for their expertise have greater chances of recognition, thus resulting in cross-pollination of learning communities'. Important in these networks are weak ties, that is, links or bridges that allow short connections between disparate ideas and fields, resulting in new innovations.

Connectivism then offers an integration of principles introduced within chaos, network, complexity and self-organisation theories. Learning (defined as actionable knowledge) can reside outside of ourselves (within an organisation or a database); it is about connecting specialised information sets. Siemens sees decision making as in itself a learning process and that learning and knowledge rests in accessing a diversity of opinions. Learning how to learn through networks is more important than our 'current state of knowing' so that nurturing and maintaining connections is needed to facilitate continual learning. This line of argument sounds like CoP theory, but while Siemens is interested in the networked nodes of learning he is more interested than Wenger in the individual's relationship to the network and the knowledge and skills that the individual possesses.

Why has this view of learning been influential?

It captures a much wider debate about 21st-century learning and the skills needed for the information age. Like CoP, it has been put forward clearly and well-publicised through blogs and papers. It has been given practical application too, for example in Downes's and Siemens's work in developing large, connectivist informed, open, online courses (cMOOCs), including a seminal course on 'Connectivism and Connectivist Knowledge', or CCK08, in 2008.

What problems are there with connectivism?

It is a provocative paper presented in rhetorical style but characteristic of much writing about technology it is dismissive of what came before and quick to foresee revolutions in learning. It is not at all clear why past learning theory is outdated; the context for learning changes but the metaphors we use to describe learning are arguably transferrable. In particular, it is not clear why a theory of social constructivism, with its interest in language and collaboration, could not be adapted for contemporary settings. To be fair, Siemens usefully sees learning as an individual undertaking in a networked environment but he does not offer an adequate theory of how we come to make sense of all this new information. As learners we need to be noticing patterns but who can help us do this? As with much social learning with technology literature there are questions about the status of knowledge we create in communities. Those excited by networked technologies were understandably focused on the opportunities for sharing and developing knowledge in a kind of free marketplace of ideas. Sadly, this seems quite utopian today when so much networked media are owned and manipulated. Even when say fellow professionals come together in closed groups to share knowledge and expertise how do we know that they are operating on democratic principles?

Do we need theory in an age of Big Data?

Finally, we should add a word on learning analytics as an alternative to learning theory. The thinking here is that we do not need to think deeply about learning theory with the emergence of 'Big Data' (this is usually associated with the three Vs: increasing *volumes* and *varieties* of data which are being processed in real time or at a *velocity* not seen before). Big Data applications have become routine in the organisation of industry, health, crisis management, city planning and so on, but education has been slower to take advantage and this is something that learning analytics (LA) has sought to address. LA has been focused on the mass of data generated in online environments, most often within learning platforms, but also in electronically monitored physical settings, including classrooms and physical libraries. If we combine these digital data on learner activity with more static data on learners' demographic characteristics, retention and grades then it might be possible to construct predictive models not only to describe learning outcomes after the event but to enable 'just in time' action to support particular groups of students as and when they need it (see Jovanović et al, 2021).

To some degree LA looks and feels like behaviourism as what matters is the modelling of inputs and outputs and not the experiences of learners or teachers. However, many case studies could better be described as atheoretical as they make little or no reference to learning theory at all. An example of the predictive modelling approach is a study by Hung et al (2019) which looked at whether LA could assist in the early identification of at-risk students. Using a mix of static data, in which gender became the key focus, and dynamic data, the frequency with which course material was accessed online and the number of contributions posted, the aim was to provide a model for successful or at-risk pathways. This study looked at two datasets, one covering learners in higher education, where the use of VLEs is much more established, and the other learners in a school. The study found that identifying those who were not accessing course material or contributing to online discussions could help point to those at risk of failing, but any model operated differently in different kinds of course, for example discussion-heavy as against content-heavy courses.

Studies such as Hung et al have provided some useful insights into learner behaviour and learning outcomes but the goal of providing reliable, predictive and hence transferable models has not been achieved. One reason for this is that while researchers can easily, and often automatically, capture online activity, these data are not always the most important when it came to explaining successful outcomes (see, for example, Wilson et al, 2017). Indeed, in any kind of learning there is a lot going in physical spaces, such as classrooms, cafes, ad hoc study spaces in the home and so on, which is not easily recorded. Moreover, if we only research people by their actions then we miss the internal properties that make people who they are, for example, we miss their motivation and their sense of learner identity, which are so crucial to explaining outcomes.

Of course, sources of digital data are constantly growing. It is possible to capture data about library visits, use of leisure facilities and, in theory, huge amounts of data could be made available to researchers if they had constant access to students' mobile phones. Work has also been carried out using eye tracking and gesture analysis to measure engagement; sensors and wearable trackers can capture movement; and even scanning of brain activity can come into research (see Drachsler and Schneider, 2018). If ethical concerns over surveillance were overcome, researchers could access a lot more besides, but would this result in data-rich predictive models of learning? Certainly, it might provide some insights but crude LA flies in the face of accepted research practice: when it comes to statistical testing researchers should articulate hypotheses in advance, not go fishing for associations by trial and error. Further, there are simply so many different kinds of courses that it seems unlikely that really reliable generalised models are possible.

Summary

In this chapter I have:

- suggested that learning theories provide a lens on what is happening and come with strengths and shortcomings;
- discussed the importance of collaboration in theories of learning with networked technology;
- described learning theories as 'big' or 'middle range'; and
- identified difficulties in atheoretical descriptions of learning.

Where to read more

There are a range of books and articles dealing with traditional learning theory. Illeris (2018) is one out of many articles on the history of these theories with a particular interest in adult learning including transformative and experiential theories. There is a lot written on Vygotsky, including several biographies which provide useful background (for example, Yasnitsky, 2018).

I have not explicitly discussed action-oriented approaches in terms of learning theory and instead cover participatory research in Chapter 5 (for example, Bentley et al, 2019; Razzouk and Shute, 2012) and looked at action research in Chapter 1 (for example, Pitura and Terlecka-Pacut, 2018). Theories of action learning often draw on Dewey, Lewin and the 'emancipatory' methodology of Freire. For more on Dewey, whose action-oriented theory, informed knowledge building and CoI approaches, see Dewey (1916/1947) and the biography written by Ryan (1995). I have discussed the theoretical underpinning of action research in more detail in Hammond (2013). The idea of joining a learning club presented in this chapter is a reference back to Smith (1988).

One of the earliest, but nonetheless key, texts on learning theory in networked times is that of Salomon (1993), *Distributed cognitions*. It includes both Salomon's and Pea's chapters which are already cited in this chapter as well as an introduction to activity theory, which is covered in Chapter 6. Lave and Wenger write very clearly on community and learning (for example, Lave, 1977; Lave and Wenger, 1991; Wenger, 1998) and this is perhaps one reason for their popularity. Chan and van Aalst (2018) is a good overview of KB and raises general questions about knowledge and group processes. Swan and Ice (2010) present several perspectives on the CoI framework.

There is much more on learning analytics than can be covered in this book. For more, go to special editions of journals (for example, Haythornthwaite et al, 2013; Martin and Sherin, 2013; Drachsler and Schneider, 2018). Jovanovic et al (2021) provide a useful contextualisation of learning analytics and an insightful case study.

4

Teachers and technology: why does take-up seem so difficult?

In Chapter 3 we looked at the ways in which learning theory could provide a lens on the use of digital technology but this is not going to be helpful if technology itself is not being taken up very much in schools, colleges or universities in the first place. In fact, there is an often-reported paradox: technology seems to offer considerable benefits to teachers and learners, teachers are generally keen, or say they are keen, on using it and learners seem motivated by using it so why does technology seem so little used in practice? We turn to looking at ways in which researchers have tried to explain this 'paradox'. The chapter is divided into five sections:

- Listing the factors: an under-theorised approach
- What do we know about school leadership and school reform?
- Activity theory (a framework on practice)
- Ecological approaches
- Theories compared

Listing the factors: an under-theorised approach

When computers were first being introduced in schools, at least into those educational systems which could afford them, understanding the take-up of technology did not seem such a difficult issue. The problem was primarily one of access: there were more teachers wanting to use the machines than machines available. As access grew so would use in the classroom. Research could still be carried out, but this was more about mapping the use of particular tools, for example, showing how to support the revising and editing of writing using a word processor, how to organise groups when working on Logo, how to make use of databases and spreadsheets for interrogating large sets of data and so on. Yet as access grew there were still problems with adoption and it was being noted that computer use by teachers was sporadic and tended to be used for 'supplementary activities'. Moreover, those supporting computers in education had long argued their use would lead to changes in teaching methods and in ways of accessing information (for example, Watson, 2001). However, such a transformative impact was difficult to detect.

There were then two problems about take-up: technology was not being used enough and technology was not being used as intended. In trying to get to the root of these problems it was natural to look at teachers who did adopt computers and compare with those who held back. An early contribution came from a survey of secondary teachers in the United States (Becker, 1994), which found both contextual and personal factors were associated with 'exemplary' use (exemplary was a complex construct which included frequency of use and goals for use). In terms of contextual issues, exemplary teachers were more likely to work in collegiate schools and ones in which more investment had been made in staff development. Complementary to this were personal factors including past training and interest in pedagogy, engagement with subject content, and a greater willingness to develop group work and other more innovative approaches. Exemplary teachers were also more likely to be male and had been teaching for longer.

Many other studies have, like Becker, reported on the factors which influence ICT use and these have included age ('digital nativism'), gender and attitude to professional development – though, to this day, much less is known about whether teachers of particular subjects, or teachers within primary, secondary and tertiary phases, are more likely to use technology than others. The link between ICT use and pedagogical orientation has also been shown in some studies (for example, Sang et al, 2010). Equally important are beliefs about the nature of knowledge, that is, teachers with a more pragmatic idea of knowledge were more likely to embrace the opportunities provided by internet technology than those who saw knowledge as contained within defined subject fields and adequately captured in textbooks (see, for example, John, 2005). All this work was informative, but very piecemeal, and in looking at factors impacting on take-up it was inevitable that some researchers turned towards TAM inventories (see Davis, 1989) to provide a theoretical weight to their work. These often showed an association between readiness to use digital tools and perception of their usefulness and ease of use (for example, Teo and Milutinovic, 2015; Sadaf et al, 2016).

Interesting as what I have called the factors approach to ICT take-up has been, it is striking how difficult it is to draw firm conclusions about teacher characteristics and take-up. For example, an early gender divide appeared but is now much less in evidence, the link between social constructivist beliefs and ICT use became hard to detect when more instructional software such as IWBs and VLEs became mainstream, and the idea that younger teachers ('digital natives') entering the profession were more likely to be frequent users of ICT in the classroom did not materialise. There was also once an interest in 'technophobia' as an issue, but this has now largely disappeared, albeit teachers' technological confidence and competence are still seen as possible personal factors in the decision to use ICT.

One gap in the research of factors is that it underplays the context in which teachers work. Here, the key issue in many systems has been and remains that of access. This is particularly felt in locations, of which there are great many, in which access to electricity is limited, let alone access to computers and to the internet (see, for example, Hennessy et al, 2010). Moreover, even when computers and technology are available there are questions as to whether they are maintained adequately and whether there are support systems in place for teachers. But let us imagine that all the problems of access have been addressed, in such a world those teachers keen on the use of digital tools would still not be free to do as they wish; they would be influenced by subject cultures in their institutions and their work would be framed by schemes of work and curriculum assessment. So both context and personal characteristics matter – though it is one thing noting the importance of both, but another to say which is more important. In this respect, Ertmer (2005) described context issues such as access, time for preparation, facilities, curriculum, training and support as first-order factors, while personal characteristics, such as orientation to subject and to pedagogy, levels of competence and confidence with technology, were second-order. Ertmer argued (and this was written about in the United States and not the developing world) that second-order factors were becoming the key issue as access had increased so markedly.

The factors approach tends to present a static view of ICT take-up and struggles to explain change. Looking for a more theoretical basis some researchers, and indeed policy makers, latched onto Rogers's (2010) 'Diffusion of Innovations' (DoI). Rogers's work had an overlap with TAM in that he saw that decisions about adoption were based, to some extent, on users' perceptions of the possible gains associated with an innovation, the complexity of learning any associated new system, and the observed effects on the organisation. However, he had a stronger interest in the change process than Davis and the innovations that interested Rogers were not confined to technology. Rogers also looked for wider factors – he recognised that the community and market exerted pressure for change – and saw the process of adoption as a weighing up of pros and cons. For example, an innovation may be complex but if it really did improve on existing systems then it might still be adopted.

Rogers saw innovations as passing through stages covering: *knowledge*; *persuasion*; *decision*; *implementation*; and *confirmation*. Moreover, Rogers was interested in the characteristics of individuals in an organisation who might help or hold back the process. He noted that people would adopt changes at different rates and provided a typology of reactions to innovation consisting of *innovators*; *early adopters*; *early majority*; *late majority*; and *laggards*. In brief, innovators were willing to take more risks and had resources to better enable them to carry those risks. Early adopters were more cautious but their steadiness made them influential as opinion leaders and in getting other people on board. Early majority adopters wanted to see how well the innovation was going in practice before they got started. They were not resistant in principle and tended to adopt before others, but they were not leading the change either. The late majority, in contrast, tended to be sceptical and needed support and a clear nudge if they were to innovate. Finally, came the laggards who would hold out as long as possible before taking on an innovation and then only do so reluctantly and half-heartedly. The traits of the individual were important in this typology so that people who were motivated and flexible, even if a minority, might be important opinion formers in their organisations. The hope was that at some point there would be a critical mass of adopters so that the use of the system became routine.

Rogers presented a dynamic picture of change and this gave encouragement to those who hoped that they were seeing the take-up of technology by innovators and early adopters, something that would lead to later widescale adoption. But perhaps Rogers, or at least the way DoI was being interpreted, was overly optimistic. More to the point, perhaps it was the transferability of DoI, and other models developed in commercial organisations, into education that needed to be questioned. In the commercial world there is a market logic that drives technology use, it will be adopted if it keeps costs down. Education has diverse and competing goals and historically at least a degree of autonomy both for schools and for teachers within them. Schools have what Hodkinson and Hodkinson (2003) describe as 'secret stories' which make them resistant to official discourses about teaching and teachers offer their own interpretations of their work and the ways in which they evaluate learners and learning. This leads us to suspect that we need a more distinctively educational perspective on school reform.

What do we know about school leadership and school reform?

One key voice interested in the constraints on the take-up of ICT was Larry Cuban (1986, 2001; Cuban et al, 2001). Cuban was interested in school reform and school leadership before he became interested in computers and from this vantage point he argued that both policy makers and educational researchers had put too much faith in technology as a solution to the problems that affected education. He argued not against computers in schools per se, though that was not always the impression a reader may get, but that we should be realistic about their impact. When one took a long view one could see a repeated pattern of over-expectation when it came to technology. For example, educational radio and television were once seen as offering unparalleled opportunities for engaging students and presaging a revolution in learning. Yet their influence was minor and classroom teaching went on much as before. We can add here that it was once expected that listening to gramophone discs, and mimicking what we had heard, would help us all to become fluent in second languages and when that failed to happen language laboratories, in which students listened to taped dialogues and practised oral drills, would lead to a further language learning revolution. In the event results were disappointing (Keating, 1963). And so it was with computers in schools – they were not changing the shape of teaching and learning, in fact, they were having limited impact. Cuban (see Case 4.1) argued that change would not happen as long as schools were organised around timetabled lessons and the teacher role was that of content knowledge mediator. This was a message picked up in other studies including reporting on how new teachers lost their enthusiasm for ICT once they got to work in controlled educational systems (for example, Levin and Wadmany, 2005) and would later explain the lack of impact that 'digital native' teachers were making.

Case 4.1: High access and low use of technologies in high school classrooms: explaining an apparent paradox (Cuban et al, 2001)

What is this study about?

This study arose to address a question: why had computers had so little influence in school? The traditional answer was in terms of access to machines, but Cuban and colleagues researched two schools in Silicon Valley (a name given to an area of California, USA, in which many high-tech companies are located) in which there was, at the time of the study, comparatively good access to computers, with better access at home, and a high degree of knowledge and support for computing among parents. Teachers had positive attitudes towards computers, appeared willing to use them in school and were often regular computer users in their personal lives. They valued computers for making their work easier and their teaching more engaging. For example, their planning was more efficient, they often communicated with colleagues via email, and secured information from the internet for teaching. They saw their students' direct access to information as 'a phenomenal enhancement to their teaching'. Yet in spite of the strong promotion and investment in technology teachers tended to make only occasional use of computers in classrooms (less so than their use of more traditional media such as video, television programmes and overhead projectors) and only a few teachers had organised their classes differently or become more student-centred in their teaching. Indeed, when technology was used it was often for routine tasks such as presenting information.

Why had more fundamental change not happened?

One idea the authors discuss is that perhaps they were seeing emergent practices and the use of computers may yet take off in the following years so that 'small changes accumulating over time create a slow-motion transformation'. They do not completely dismiss this but point to constraints on technology in terms of shortcomings in training and support for teachers. Effective change needs early engagement of teachers, adequate levels of resourcing and an understanding of the change process. Too often teachers do not have the time to find and evaluate software. More importantly, the way that schools were structured (their timetabled lessons, departmental boundaries, external testing and the appeal that established practices had over 'policy makers, practitioners, researchers, and taxpayers') meant there was very little opportunity for teaching to be otherwise. Teachers behave as 'academic specialists whose primary concern is covering the body of information contained within a text in 36 weeks'. In such a context the influence of technology on curriculum change is almost bound to be marginal.

What is valuable about this paper?

This paper addresses a key question that was and remains core to the use of technology in education: 'Why have computers not had the influence that many had both hoped and expected?'. The answer is what happens in school needs to be seen in the context of a wider system. As such the authors inject a note of realism into the debate over technology. The paper is admirable in setting out two possible interpretations of the data – one, that restricted use of technology should be seen as emergent practice, and two, that practice will continue to be restricted. The authors plump for the second but leave open the first as a possibility.

What might be contested in the paper?

As with many papers the authors are looking for disruption of traditional schooling with technology and have taken claims of impact at face value. However, if we start with a more realistic idea of what technology can and cannot do there is evidence of impact in the paper (that is, planning was more efficient, communication was more regular and the internet provided resources for teaching). They further reported that some teachers, around a quarter, had organised their classes differently, lectured less, gave students more independence, and acted more 'like a coach than the performer on stage'. It is more complicated than, as Cuban once put it, 'computer meets school, school wins'.

Furthermore, perhaps we would get a different view if we looked at learners rather than teachers. For example, it has become natural for learners to actively search for materials online and, where allowable, they word process documents and use data handling packages as routine. They almost spontaneously set up online groups and engage in online discussion. This, as we see later, can be easily romanticised, but it offers evidence of the real influence of technology on learning.

How does this paper add to theorisation of technology take-up?

The paper is full of clear, well-supported claims and offers an explanation of low take-up in the organisation of schooling. This theorisation is helpful but is, to use the language of Chapter 2, narrow. There is a wider story to be told about organisational inertia and how structural demands are mediated by teachers – though to be fair this is just one paper and Cuban has written much more.

Cuban's and other researchers' work on the take-up of technology should be read in the context of a growing literature on school reform over the past 20 or 30 years. Here a key contribution came from Fullan's (2007 [first edition 1982]) *Meaning of educational change*. Fullan was not particularly focused on technology, though later he became an enthusiast for 'twenty first century learning' (for example, Fullan and Langworthy, 2013). Rather, he was very much interested in the wider question as to why education reform was so difficult to enact. His answer was that we needed to understand that different stakeholders (teachers, principals, students, district administrators, government policy makers and leaders) had very different perspectives on change. All had their own priorities and all worked to different timetables and this meant that communication and flexibility were important if a mutual commitment to, and understanding of, change was to be achieved. In particular, those seeking to change education must let individual schools and teachers find their own stance on any reforms being proposed. Teachers must further be provided with support and given a realistic timeframe – change should be enacted over years, not semesters. In contrast, most attempts at educational reform were hurried and top-down, with policy makers not responsive enough to local circumstances. In part, this was inevitable as policy makers were by the very nature of things focused on political expediency and short-term goals. This created a problem as change from above resulted in passive acceptance, that is, adoption of the innovation in form but not in spirit, and what looked like change may turn out not to be change at all. In fact, I can add here that there are many examples of such superficial adoption when it comes to technology. IWBs were expected to be used to support more interactive whole class teaching, but in practice have been widely used for displaying PowerPoint slides; word processing was promoted as a support for a more interactive writing process but is often used for the presentation of 'best work'; VLEs were designed with communication in mind but turned out to be more frequently used for storing teachers' presentation slides. If deep rather than superficial change is to happen then teachers need time to understand what is proposed and be given the flexibility to adapt any proposals in ways that made sense to them.

Fullan's theory of educational change came at a time when there was a new focus in school leadership studies on the culture of the organisation, rather than on the characteristics of the individuals in charge (for example, Bush and Glover, 2014). Of course, school and other leaders needed to manage on a day-to-day basis, but they also had a responsibility for creating a vision for their schools and to bring the structures, routines and activities of the school in line with the achievement of this vision. They could not do it all by themselves. There were many different ways of understanding leadership (for example, instructional, managerial, transformational, participative and other leadership styles became defined and discussed) but engagement and participation were key issues and a link was made between sustainable curriculum change and distributed leadership. The word 'distributed' has echoes with the idea of distributed learning and community of practice outlined in Chapter 2 and indeed distributed leadership theory had an interest in exploring the ways that school communities developed routines and expectations through joint participation. One aspect of this was a heightened focus on what teachers enacted together rather than on the formal roles and responsibility of senior and middle management (Spillane, 2005).

Distributed leadership calls for negotiation and a culture of interdependency and support. It is far from the only kind of leadership needed within a school but it seems particularly important in the context of technology introduction as high levels of engagement are needed if digital tools are to be used in a way that makes a difference. Distributed leadership also reflects the reality in many schools that those most able to contribute to the development of technology use may not be in formal positions of leadership. On the other hand, distributed leadership is not a panacea for the introduction of technology and the idea itself is sometimes critiqued, as is CoP, for underplaying asymmetries in power and status and assuming a level of autonomy that teachers simply may not have.

Running parallel to this renewed interest in the culture of schools and shared if not distributed leadership was a reconsideration of the nature of continuing professional development (CPD). In the past, CPD was discussed in relation to one-off programmes of in-service and pre-service training, something to be 'delivered' to teachers. In contrast, later researchers wanted to elevate the importance of everyday participation of staff in their schools when it came to teacher development and Day offered a much-cited definition of CPD as consisting of:

> all the natural learning experience and those conscious and planned activities which are intended to be of direct or indirect benefit to the individual, group or school, which contribute, through these, to the quality of education in the classroom. It is the process by which, alone and with others, teachers review, renew and extend their commitment as change agents to the moral purpose of teaching; and by which they acquire and develop critically the knowledge, skills, and emotional intelligence essential to good professional thinking, planning and practice with children, young people and colleagues throughout each phase of their teaching lives. (Day, 1999: 4)

This broadens the idea of CPD to take in both formal (taught sessions) and informal (for example, conversations struck up between teachers) activities. A further distinction is between *planned* (for example, the intention to try out a new activity in the classroom) and *spontaneous* (for example, a sudden realisation of a possible solution to a problem) opportunities for development. Of course, in practice the distinctions may not be clear-cut.

This wider understanding of CPD is important as it suggests that the impact of taught CPD sessions can be minimal if teachers are not supported with a collaborative school culture when it comes to innovation and changes in practice. Day's definition of CPD further speaks to the agenda of teacher engagement as teachers are expected to 'review, renew and extend' their commitment to change and to have a critical understanding of the purpose of an innovation. This recognises the importance of teacher agency but, as with distributed leadership theory, could be critiqued for offering an overly benign view of school and the level of autonomy open to teachers.

Activity theory (a framework on practice)

Having looked at what we know about education reform, I turn now to a more general theory that has been used to account for the take-up, or non-take-up, of technology. This is activity theory, or cultural historical activity theory (CHAT) as it is often called. Cole and Engeström (1993) provide a short introduction. They start by drawing on Vygotsky to argue that the crucial difference between human beings and animals is that humans can make use of tools. This is, of course, far from an original observation but their particular angle was that tools (both material and symbolic) not only help people to achieve their goals but 'react on them' and change their 'physic condition', in particular tools can act as a support for, or in their absence a constraint on, thinking. More precisely tools mediate between the person (*subject*) and what they want to achieve (*object*) in a way already set out in the discussion of social constructivism in Chapter 2. One consequence of this mediation is that it allows us to access past cultural achievements and past ways of thinking to achieve new goals. Indeed, such is the influence of the past that we can only achieve what is possible within the cultural and material context in which we live.

Once we think about goals as socially mediated we can focus on the uses to which tools are put, for example, a stick may provide support for helping us walk but we can easily imagine other uses too, depending on context. However, tools find a home depending on not just the individual goals the user has but how the user has been influenced by *community* expectations and constrained by the *rules* in place (these can include informal institutional practices as well as contractual rules). Both rules and community expectations can be difficult to dislodge. In discussing community, Cole and Engeström are further interested in the *division of labour* within an institution or 'who is expected to do what'. This leads them to present a framework (CHAT) with six key elements: subject; object; rules; community; division of labour; mediating artefacts (see Figure 4.1). Thus, if an earlier complaint I made against social constructivist learning theory (see Table 4.1) was that it was too focused on the micro level, then CHAT provides a more holistic view of activity. This is exemplified in Cole and Engeström not through the application of technology but with an example of the take-up of a new reading scheme. Here they found individual readers were influenced by their community (or reading groups); by their formal roles in groups; and by following implicit rules of instruction.

The value of CHAT and the reason for its take-up in discussing technology is that it pushes researchers to think not only about the perspectives or characteristics of teachers (though this would be important), but also the goals (or objects) of a teacher, or indeed learner, within a wider system. This is its key strength. In addition, CHAT helps researchers focus on contradictions within the system. For example, all kinds of disruption to education systems are possible when computers are introduced but if roles and rules are unchanged these disruptive opportunities are unlikely to be acted upon.

There are, as ever, drawbacks to consider and a weakness of CHAT is that the focus on the system as a whole can be methodologically overwhelming; just how can you write a coherent account of change that takes in so many foci? Further, those using CHAT can end up over-interpreting it, and here the triangles within triangles in Figure 4.1, which was intended as a loose framework, became seen by some almost as a model of causality with five elements acting upon the subject and defining what is possible. This led critics to complain that the individual was not seen as having agency in

Figure 4.1: The basic mediational triangle in cultural historical activity theory

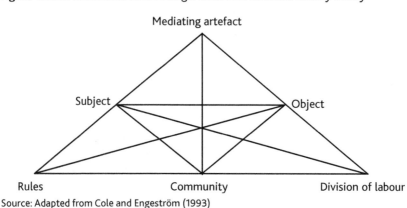

Source: Adapted from Cole and Engeström (1993)

CHAT and that the CHAT approach led us to view systems as static. This was a criticism which Engeström (2001) sought to address. He stood by the idea that activity needed to be analysed in the context of a system. However, rather than seeing the activity system as 'one all-encompassing immovable thing', he argued that 'it was always capable of renegotiation'. Of particular importance were contradictions in the system. Contradictions can 'aggravate' the system, they generate disturbances and conflicts, and at times innovation. The system might not be as fixed as stakeholders think and small changes could lead to more people beginning to question the system and deviating from community norms. All this might lead to an 'expansive transformation' once 'the object and motive of the activity are reconceptualized to embrace a radically wider horizon of possibilities than in the previous mode of the activity. A full cycle of expansive transformation may be understood as a collective journey through the zone of proximal development of the activity' (Engeström, 2001: 137).

In spite of this expansive potential, CHAT has been used repeatedly to explain how technology innovations lose their disruptive power once they are introduced into education. For example, designers of prototype VLEs envisaged them as disruptive, they were content-free containers in which learners could upload resources for sharing and post ideas for discussion, a kind of academic Facebook. Teachers could, of course, provide their own content too, but perhaps this could form part of a blended learning solution in which students accessed material outside of class time and used F2F teaching time for discussion, including group work. In this way, VLEs, like much other technology introduced into education, had the potential to disrupt 'traditional' or instructional teaching and learning and replace it with something more collaborative and free-flowing. In practice, such disruption rarely happened and in many cases VLEs ended up as little more than repositories for PowerPoint slides and for managing attendance and assessment.

From the CHAT perspective such disappointing outcomes are not surprising, after all here is a system with rules and a community which might be too constrained to allow a rethinking of pedagogy. As an example, in one study Blin and Munro (2008) explored a university in Ireland and found that while the use of the VLE was widespread, this had caused little pedagogic disruption. Indeed, the materials which had been added to the VLE were 'static', that is, content-based resources such as web pages and lecture notes. Assessment methods had not changed either and 'activities that demanded collaboration or reflection, such as glossaries, journals, and wikis were used less frequently than those that replicated face-to-face teaching modes' (Blin and Munro, 2008: 488). Why was this? There were particular issues worth exploring, including the nature of training provided for staff, but overall one had to look at the activity system. Or rather two systems. For there was a technological system with a logic of its own in terms of tools, rules, division of labour and so on, running alongside a well-established semiotic system with its existing division of labour, rules and community. The technological system could not shift the semiotic system in a finding that echoed Cuban's adage 'computer meets school, school wins'.

However, I am in danger of offering too static a view of CHAT and Blin and Appel (2011) present a more expansive study by looking at language learners' use of online synchronous forums. This study shows that learners did take opportunities for collaboration and were able to begin creating and discussing joint artefacts. The authors note the importance of the tools in the activity system but also the role of the teachers in shifting learners' attention so that they could better work together. Collaboration was still constrained but overall CHAT appeared as a more fluid concept in this study, in particular it was possible to see the emerging practices which digital tools allowed.

Ecological approaches

Both Cuban and Engeström offer environmental views of system change but not quite a full-blown ecological perspective in which Bronfenbrenner's (1979) ecological theory is often a point of reference. Bronfenbrenner was interested in child development and addressed the age-old nature versus nurture debate, that is, were life chances a consequence of individual characteristics or a consequence of upbringing and environment? He saw, drawing on personal experience, that the role of the environment had been historically underplayed and argued that child development took place in nested systems with different levels of influence. In brief, these different levels covered a *micro* system such as a family or classroom which the child experienced directly; a *meso* system in which various micro systems interacted without the child present, for example, a parent meeting a teacher; and an *exo* system which was external to the child, but directly influenced those with whom the child interacted, for example, the way parenting might be affected by a parent losing a job. At a more removed level was a *macro* system consisting of policies and discourse around childhood. Finally, there was a *chrono* system which took account of change over time.

Bronfenbrenner's idea, elaborated more forcefully in later work, was to see the child as in a state of active development as they navigated a path through these different systems. Bronfenbrenner is then helpful not just in understanding child development but in providing ways of thinking about social life more generally as he captures both the subjective and objective quality of the worlds in which we live. Actors have their own perspective on the world and are able to express agency at the micro level, but they are also up against an objective social and material reality which includes systems which they cannot directly influence.

Adapting from Bronfenbrenner it is possible to see teachers as enfolded in different layers of influence. The micro system of the classroom is a direct and compelling environment for expressing values (such as a belief in learner-centred pedagogy) and interests (such as the possible use of technology to extend learning). However, teachers' work is nested within a set of further interactions. For example, teachers work on documents and artefacts with colleagues and leadership teams at a meso level, but schemes of work and systems of assessment might be mandated by school consortia, education authorities and departments of education at a more removed macro level.

It is essential to understand that teachers work within a wider ecology as it is unrealistic to expect change to happen if the various layers of the system are not aligned. It is no good, for example, expecting teacher-led change at a micro level, or alternatively mandated top-down change at the macro level, to work if computer use is not negotiated and built into schemes of work at the meso level. In fact, when it comes to technology, very often the layers are not aligned and, as with Fullan, ecological theory tells us it is particularly important that policy makers are responsive to what is happening at the micro level and let practice adapt accordingly.

Several writers have introduced a specifically ecological approach to their research of technology in education, albeit not always drawing explicitly on Bronfenbrenner. For example, Davis et al (2019) offered a model for the take-up of ICT in which the classroom was nested within school, district, state, national and global systems. This is illustrated in an 'arena framework' in which teachers and parents are critical (to use an ecological analogy they are described as the 'keystone species') but their actions are mediated within a wider system of both digital products and social institutions. In a second example, Rana et al (2020) looked at ICT integration in a developing country, that of Nepal, and they found a complicated ecology. In particular, there was a disconnect between aspirational policies around ICT and its non-use in schools. From an ecological point of view the system did not join up. In particular, in rural schools there were not only low levels of CPD and support for teachers but access was a further, and particularly important, constraint not just access to computers but also to the internet and to a reliable electricity supply. Gaps in access were filled by non-government organisations, but only partially, and their role was double-edged, offering resources and support but also creating complications for the planning and running of the education system in general.

A further framework for understanding the ecological dimension to tool use comes from Valsiner (1997). Valsiner is best known for a 'zones framework', first developed through a detailed examination of Vygotsky's social cultural theory (see Chapter 2). Put briefly, the framework sees human activity as taking place within three zones: the Zone of Free Movement (ZFM), the Zone of Promoted Action (ZPA) and the Zone of Proximal

Development (ZPD). The ZFM defines possibilities: 'what is available to the person acting in a particular environment at a given time'. In this sense a zone of free movement is a little misleading; a ZFM is a zone of constraint as well as opportunity. The ZPA defines what, in respect to the person's actions, is being promoted. The ZPD, borrowed from Vygotsky, defines possible next steps in the person's relationship with his or her environment. The ZPD works within the boundaries set up by the ZFM/ZPA system. Valsiner argues the crossing of the ZPD can be carried out without direct help, but individual agency by itself is not enough; social interaction is needed to 'canalise' activity. 'Canalisation' is a key term and is used to describe how activity is framed or channelled in particular ways within the three zones. For example, it is difficult to canalise proposals for action if they lie at the margins of an actor's ZPD, or if these proposals are jostling for space within a very broad ZFM.

The zones framework is, like the work of Bronfenbrenner, an example of theory developed in the study of child development being put to more general use. For some, the idea of zones offers a particularly useful metaphor for the use of ICT as it prompts researchers to ask how far the use of technology can become settled in schools and other institutions. For example, the use of statistical packages such as SPSS, and now Python programming, became standard features of courses on data handling, at least at tertiary level, and as they were promoted in the curriculum and now lie firmly within many university teachers' ZPD. In contrast, live classes were very rarely used in most educational systems as they were not heavily promoted, their use lay outside most teachers' ZPD, and teachers could ignore them if they had enough 'free movement' to do so. Of course, in COVID-19-related lockdown the picture changed and live classes became heavily promoted, even mandated, in order of provide remote teaching. But this was with mixed results, one reason being that teachers were often expected to find out for themselves how to use live class software (they continued to operate within a very broad ZFM) and in many cases the programmes were new and remained at the margins of their ZPD.

Theories compared

I have looked at four ways of understanding change and technology (see Table 4.1). Each comes with strengths and constraints.

First, the 'factors approach' was seen as providing important insights into just how varied teacher responses to the use of technology are and, up to a point, shows that there are some contextual factors limiting technology use. However, it has left important gaps. It has not offered a dynamic picture, too often providing snapshots rather than narratives of change. Methodologically, the factors approach lends itself to surveys and self-reporting rather than

Table 4.1: Value and shortcomings of different theories of change in educational use of technology

Approach	What is it?	Value	Shortcomings	Theoretical underpinning
Factors approach	Largely descriptive research noting how personal characteristics influence ICT take-up; extended into how first order factors such as access, training and curriculum play a role	Shows teachers are not uniform when responding to ICT; allows a focus on early adopters; can be flexible enough to consider both teacher and context	Tends to underplay context; may result in lists rather than explanatory models; offers a static view of the system	Often descriptive rather than theoretically rich; TAM and DoI seen as useful frameworks
Educational systems	Looks at the challenge of reforming education; brings in new concepts of leadership and CPD	Explains why many attempts at reform fail; shows how education systems are distinctive; provides a blueprint for iterative sustainable change	Can appear out of kilter at a time when policy is increasingly mandated; can underplay asymmetry in terms of power and influence within the system	Generally underpinned by 'middle range' typologies of leadership and CPD; develops concepts such as distributed leadership and models of CPD
CHAT	An activity system shows how opportunities for action are shaped by rules, community, division of labour; a general framework not specifically developed for education	Presents a holistic picture of an organisation; has a helpful focus on tools; can help diagnose blockages and contradictions within a system; an expansive version of CHAT can address some earlier weaknesses	The 'triangles within triangles' model can be over interpreted; the framework can be complex; people (subjects) can be lost in the system	Vygotsky and tradition of social constructionism
Ecological	Shows that innovation is carried out across different layers or fields; transferred from child development studies into education studies	Shows the interaction of the person and the context in subtle ways; points to the need to align different systems to bring about change	As a social psychology approach it does not provide tools for understanding policy and wider discourses about education	Bronfenbrenner; Valsiner and field theory

observation of practice. As an approach it is often descriptive rather than theoretically informed. DoI theory does help here but it is not clear how far this should be applied to education systems.

Second, thinking of schools (and other educational institutions) as distinctive kinds of organisations was seen as addressing gaps in the factors approach. In particular, it showed that innovation in general is complex, and requires commitment, support and a sophisticated understanding of the change process. Indeed, much of the literature on technology seems to exist in a bubble. If we took more time to understand schools and school leadership in general we would see that all educational change is difficult, not just technology take-up. Furthermore, by understanding the change process we might become aware of an important tension in the promotion of technology summed up in the idea that 'teachers need time and support to find their own perspective on technology use, if they are to use it properly'. This is fine, but what is 'proper use'? For education reformers 'proper' often means more group-based, exploratory learning. But we cannot have it both ways. *Either* teachers find their own perspectives on technology *or* they get told how to use it 'properly'.

Next, I moved onto more social psychological approaches to understanding institutional change and development. CHAT was not developed with computers or schools specifically in mind but has been imaginatively adapted in education research to show how teachers work within a wider system of opportunity and constraint. For whatever reason CHAT has sometimes been interpreted rather deterministically, but CHAT is capable of more flexible ('expansive') interpretation. Nonetheless, those working in this tradition need to be careful not to get overwhelmed by the comprehensiveness of the model and lose the voice of the teacher (the subject) in the system.

Finally, ecological approaches derived from Bronfenbrenner, Valsiner and others were seen as more flexible alternatives to CHAT and offered imaginative metaphors (nested layers, zones and fields) for the influence of the wider system on the teacher. Ecological approaches show the tensions and opportunities open to the teacher and the need to align different layers of a system to bring about change. However, researchers have not always been able to show how layers interact with each other and with what effect.

The four approaches to teacher take-up discussed here are wrestling in one way or another with how much weight should be given to teacher agency as against cultural practice and environmental constraint. They do not provide definitive answers but they help us know where to look. The clear message is that if we imagine the use of technology is largely voluntary, or that the use of technology is going to become widespread through a process of osmosis, then we are clearly wrong. We have to understand change in the context of a wider ecology, and the distinctive characteristics of an educational system.

Summary

This chapter has taken us through ways of theorising teachers and technology and I have:

- shown that the low impact of technology on teaching and learning has been explained in different ways;
- suggested that teacher actions need to be understood in the context of schools as systems or ecologies;
- presented ecological frameworks to offer dynamic views of change; and
- argued that theories need to be adapted to the contexts in which research takes place.

Where to read more

Becker (1994) and Ertmer (2005), cited in the chapter, are useful historical points of reference if looking at the factors approach to ICT take-up. Within this tradition are a great many quantitative studies exploring associations between use of ICT and variables such as gender, teaching experience and age. As an example, Tou et al (2020) looked at physical education teachers in Singapore and their attitudes to ICT broken down by gender, age, teaching experience and school level, and Petko et al (2018) provide an example of structural equation modelling, focused on teacher readiness to use ICT in Swiss primary school. In addition, Tondeur has looked at teacher beliefs and computer use (for example, Tondeur et al, 2017). In respect to gender, earlier research suggested imbalance in attitudes and use (for example, Jamieson-Proctor et al, 2006) but as noted in the chapter this is not always observed today (though see Tou et al, 2020).

There are more flexible applications of the factors approach, including Lim et al (2020) looking at education in Sri Lanka. Researchers have also looked at factors affecting take-up of technology among learners. Examples include Dimopoulos et al (2021), covering educational advantage and disadvantage in European countries, and Khlaif et al (2021), a case study of learners in Palestine. Both address learner reactions to remote teaching during the COVID-19-related school lockdowns.

Cuban's work (for example, Cuban, 1986, 2001) is always very readable as is the introduction to CHAT in Cole and Engeström (1993). It is not difficult to find CHAT case studies. Siyahhan et al (2010) is an interesting example as it concerns a 3D educational computer game, played by parents and children in an after-school club rather than a formal classroom.

Arnott et al (2019) offer an example of an ecological approach looking at the use of tools in an early learning context. Davis (2017) provides a good introduction to her Arena framework, with the message that it is important to see the wider context. For more on Valsiner, try Blanton et al (2005), Goos (2005) and my co-authored article (Hammond and Alotaibi, 2017).

Education reform, leadership and CPD all became hot topics in education and in addition to Bush and Spillane cited in the chapter, Leithwood et al (2008) and Hargreaves (cited in Chapter 2) are helpful. Darling-Hammond and Oakes (2021) offer an introductory text to teacher development.

5

A theory of technology

I have now looked at theories that have emerged, first, to explain the contribution of technology to learning and, second, how teachers use technology. In this chapter I turn to technology itself. In an obvious way the whole book has been about technology but technology deserves a chapter in itself as researchers have not always been explicit or consistent when discussing the user's relationship to digital tools. There are six sections:

- What is a technocentric view of technology?
- The idea of an affordance
- We live in hybrid environments
- We participate in assemblages of people and objects
- The social shaping of technology
- Is the important question: 'what ought technology to be?'
- How then should we think about technology?

What is a technocentric view of technology?

The use of a tool will always be influenced by who is using it and the purposes they have in mind, but a technocentric view assumes that there is something invariant, something that remains constant, even as it is used across different contexts. This often means that technocentric writers will see tools as having a power to both disrupt and change existing practice. For example, technocentric writers may see great historical movements as *caused* by technology inventions: the Enlightenment was *made possible* by the printing press; the steam engine literally *powered* the industrial revolution; the internet *created* the Information Age.

When it comes to education, policy makers have often veered towards a technocentric view of ICT, seeing it as a solution to problems such as access to education, inequality in outcomes and gaps in vocational preparation. Thus, they have often prioritised getting the equipment in schools (and other institutions), believing that this will make a difference, while giving less thought to the support and resources needed for teachers to use new technology on their own terms. A technocentric view, further, distorts the way that technology is evaluated. If we believe that ICT has invariant features then it makes sense to treat it as an 'independent variable' and to measure its impact on learning, not worrying too much about the differing contexts in which it is used. This approach is, of course, highly problematic but more understandable if evaluating a programme that is expected to be used in a laboratory setting without teacher mediation (see Case 5.1; Banerjee et al, 2007). But most use of digital tools requires teacher mediation and practice will look different depending on the classroom and the learners. Perhaps, it makes as much sense as to generalise about the impact of digital tools as to ask whether books have an impact on learning. The answer is always 'it depends'.

Case 5.1: Remedying education: evidence from two randomised experiments in India (Banerjee et al, 2007)

What is this article about?

This is a paper describing two initiatives supported by a non-government organisation working in cooperation with government schools in regions of India. The aim of these interventions was to address low learning outcomes of young children so that at the time of the study a national survey had found that '41% of the children of primary school age cannot read a simple paragraph, 56% cannot write, and 63% cannot do simple additions'. The explanation given for these low levels lay in the quality of teaching (the authors note worrying levels of teacher absenteeism) and having English as the language of instruction, when it was a second language for many of the children. Moreover there was a problem of differentiation and once children got behind, it was very difficult for them to catch up.

The study reports on two interventions, one using technology, the other not. The technology intervention was a computer-assisted learning program, in which children were offered two hours of shared (children worked in pairs) computer time per week, during which they played games that involved solving mathematical problems. The programme was designed to allow the children to learn as independently as possible without instructor input. To assess the outcomes from this intervention, an experimental methodology was used, with students divided into experimental and control groups. Researchers found a significant improvement in learning among children using the computer program and this held for children at all levels of prior achievement.

What is the strength of the study?

Unlike many other examples of experimental studies, in this case the allocations were random and large scale – over 15,000 students were included – and the evaluation was carried out over two years. Experimental studies are often critiqued for being carried out away from the context of normal classroom teaching and learning, but this is more justifiable given that the programme being evaluated was designed to be used as a stand-alone tutoring system.

What are the shortcomings?

There are places where more explanation would be helpful. For example, there could be more on why it was suitable to bring in a computer program in the first place. More importantly, perhaps the study was in essence about the poor quality of classroom teaching rather than the effectiveness of the instructional material. If so, then working around teachers by excluding them from the use of technology does not sound like a sustainable long-term solution. The study feels under-theorised as it does not provide a clear explanation for the impact of the interventions. Hence, it is difficult to know what to take from this one example into other contexts. We need to have more detail as to what the programme was designed to do and what went on in student pairs that was effective.

Those following a technocentric approach often seek to define what the technology does, and this has particular appeal to policy makers and others whose job it is to promote technology and lead developments in education. An example comes from a now dated document explaining why technology was important in education. For TTA (1998: 4), ICT offered:

- Speed and automatic functions – the feature of ICT which enables routine tasks to be completed and repeated quickly, enabling teachers to demonstrate, explore or explain aspects of their subject, and allowing pupils to concentrate on thinking and on tasks such as analysing and looking for patterns within data, asking questions and looking for answers and explaining and presenting results.
- Capacity and range – the ability of ICT to access and to handle large amounts of information; change timescales and remove barriers of distance; give teachers and pupils access to historical, recent and immediate information and control over situations which would normally be outside their everyday experience.
- Provisionality – the feature of ICT which allows information to be changed easily and enables alternatives to be explored readily.
- Interactivity – the function of ICT which enables rapid and dynamic feedback and response.

The policy makers in this example were based in England and Wales but similar kinds of lists have been put together in other countries. These are not objective definitions of what technology is; computers could of course be used in many other ways than those laid out here, and for that matter for both desirable and undesirable ends. For example, interactivity could enable dynamic feedback for the learner, but it could also enable the use of mind-numbing repetitive drills; reach could enable access to hate groups as much as to educational communities; speed of access could be a serious constraint on deliberative thinking. Policy makers and researchers who inform technology adoption, then, cherry-pick their arguments but this is to be expected and even helpful if it focuses attention on what is being promoted.

Taxonomies, or lists of what technology makes possible, can be more nuanced and more helpful than those provided by policy makers. For example, Conole and Dyke (2004) provided a taxonomy of 'new' Web 2.0 technology affordances and their implications for higher education. This covered the following (paraphrased) features:

• Accessibility, that is, relatively easy access to vast amounts of information through a variety of different mechanisms.
• Speed of change: continuous reassessment of experiences which are central to living with the rapid change of late-modernity.
• Diversity: access to a vast range of diverse and different experiences such as access to subject experts, or use of simulations.
• Communication and collaboration: the potential for learning enriched by engagement with the 'other'.
• Multimodal and non-linear organisation of content allowing different routes through, and forms of, learning.

Conole and Dyke's paper differs from some policy documents, for while it attempts to promote the use of ICT it does go on to raise a number of difficulties including issues of risk, fragility and uncertainty; tensions in the search for common standards for scalability; and surveillance. Furthermore, what technology offers is contextualised within a coherent learning paradigm so that these 'affordances' of communication, speed, accessibility and so on are only useful if we understand the importance of being able to analyse large sets of information; create new forms of dialogue; and offer greater personalisation. The approach is more even-handed but nonetheless does try to nail down the use of ICT to particular functions rather than embrace its multi-faceted nature.

Other researchers have been quick to define opportunities for using software in their own subject specialisms. Webb (2008), for example, explained how ICT could allow students to understand complex science concepts, to collaborate and address areas of difficulty. She saw applications of technology in terms of modelling, carrying out practical work, authoring multimedia and video, accessing information and displaying findings. As an example of the contribution of ICT, she discusses a simulation designed to help support the teaching of force and motion. The software provides an opportunity for students to make and test predictions, and, with the help of a teacher, to reconcile any discrepancy between their prediction and their observation of the on-screen micro world. Webb is then focusing attention on how technology ought to be used and not presenting a list of ways in which it is used. Those working in other subject areas can provide similar guidance. For example, with internet technology teachers can expand the reach of language teaching as they can easily access authentic materials from a target language community, and learners can be encouraged to communicate with each other across distance (for example, Blin and Appel, 2011). Tools such as GeoGebra, Logo and other mathematical software have assisted with the visualising of complex mathematics (for example, Ng et al, 2019) and geography teachers can use mobile technology to enhance fieldwork experiences and access real-time mapping. Virtual laboratory experiences can also promote a more exploratory approach to data handling (Chang et al, 2018).

It is tempting to see all attempts at mapping technology and defining features of technology as technocentrism but we should be careful. *Educational* researchers are not sociologists, they are interested in what ought to happen with technology rather than what does happen and it is important not to mislabel this goal as naive or deterministic. However, the yearning for mapping and defining does come with unintended consequences. One problem has been a rapidly changing nomenclature. In schools we have had a movement from *IT* to *ICT* to *digital tools*, more in higher education, a move from *E-learning*, *M-learning*, *D-* or *digital learning* (see Basak et al, 2018). At times writers also bring in reworked concepts such as *Web 1.0*, *Web 2.0*, *Web 3.0*, *4.0* and so on (see Key Terms at the end of the book). These changing terms serve some purpose, for example, E-learning was seen as too tied to the use of desktop computers to support distance learning and became too narrow when it was noticed that young people carried mobile devices that enabled them to be online all the time. The introduction of M-learning then led to a discussion of collaboration and all that it offered. Yet over time it was noticed that M-learning was too narrow and better to have a general definition of D-learning or better simply to refer to the use of digital tools. However, this has left practitioners confused as to what is being talked about and given some at least the erroneous idea that with each passing phase earlier gaps and difficulties have been addressed. Like many others, I have found myself in meetings with colleagues focused on introducing digital tools and seen the conversation go round in circles as each person has their own understanding of the terms being used, and may not even be aware that there are competing definitions. The meeting ends up as a discussion of technology as a thing (what are its features?) and a belief takes root that tools will be used in a predictable way, for example learners will use mobile phones to access learning materials rather than for aimless browsing. In contrast, discussion of technology goes better when it begins with the question 'What are the problems in our courses and how, if at all, might some of the technology we have available address them?'. The conversation then becomes about technology in context rather than about technology as a solution for an ill-defined problem (Bigum, 1998).

The idea of an affordance

One alternative to taking a technocentric view is to embrace the idea of an 'affordance'. The term itself was popularised by Norman (2013) in writing about design; here it carried the idea of suggestibility, so that good design makes it clear, or suggests to the user, what an object does. Norman's examples cover everyday artefacts such as buttons which are clearly meant to be pushed or handles meant to be turned, and we could add that intuitive design has become embedded in the practice of human–computer interaction. For example, the careful use of icons was core to the early success of Apple computers: a bin was clearly meant to denote deleting or throwing away files, a folder icon looked like somewhere a file could be placed, and the file icon looked different to a folder. This is all fine, but there was an older idea of an affordance and this was presented by Gibson (1986) who used the term to describe what an environment provided or furnished, either for good or ill:

> The verb to afford is found in the dictionary, but the noun affordance is not. I have made it up. I mean by it something that refers to both the environment and the animal in a way that no existing term does. It implies the complementarity of the animal and the environment. (Gibson, 1986: 127)

An affordance in Gibson describes the relationship between an organism and an object in relation to the needs of the organism so that a tree might afford shelter from the rain, hiding from a pursuer or even sustenance if the tree provides edible fruit. The properties of the tree remain the same but the opportunities provided by the tree differ according to need. Further, the same tree might afford different things at the same time to different organisms, as ever depending on need. We might then think about an affordance as an emergent opportunity. The affordance is there, it has always been there, but it needs to be perceived to be realised. A subsidiary idea in affordance theory is that affordances provide both opportunity and constraint. These are not opposites, rather they are complementary, so, for example, a sledgehammer affords the breaking of rocks but the user is constrained by its weight – the very thing that provides the opportunity for rock-breaking in the first place (see Hammond, 2010).

Affordances have myriad applications in studies of organisations, psychology of perception, design, and workplace learning. However, and of more interest for us, is that affordance serves as a useful conceptual tool reconciling the idea that technology has objective or 'invariant' properties with the awareness that such properties are always subjectively perceived; in other words a *property objectively* exists, it is there in the artefact, but for an affordance to exist the user needs to recognise it. This means, for example, that a spreadsheet can be described in terms of certain material features such as the coding embedded in the software and how these coded instructions are processed, but it is a mistake to assume a spreadsheet is an application that can only be used in one way, most obviously for business accounting. For a mathematics teacher a spreadsheet can be a tool for (or 'a tool that affords') exploring algebraic functions, making fractals, calculating the two times table and so on. For a statistician, a spreadsheet might be a tool for running probabilistic simulations and for a physical geographer it might assist in creating models of erosion and water loss. For a learner it might merely be a grid for holding digits. Seen in this way, tools can be put to different purposes and tensions in the ways different groups or individuals see technology noted. Downes (2002), for example, suggests that children see 'playability' as a compelling affordance of the computer. In principle this is fine and is one reason why technology use is so ubiquitous across all age groups. However, playability might be at variance with the idea of 'learnability', something which teachers are naturally keen to promote: in a nutshell is the computer a tool or toy? The teacher's definition of the computer then struggles against that of the learners. Whatever the case, digital tools can be seen as useful in many, sometimes unexpected and sometimes contested, ways but their material features mean they cannot be whatever we want them to be.

The idea of affordance also has value when it comes to discussing programme design, for which the idea of complementarity tells us that there are only best fit, not ideal, solutions. For example, how many menu functions should the user of a programme be faced with? If functions are not displayed then the user will not know they are there, if there are too many the display becomes over-crowded and navigation is difficult. The designer is trying to promote comprehensive coverage without leaving the users overwhelmed, but it is an almost impossible trick to pull off. There are only compromises.

Complementarity arises when considering modes of communication too. For example, asynchronicity is a valuable feature of email and social networks as it affords the user time for reflection before responding. However, asynchronicity can also afford procrastination as there is the opportunity to endlessly put off a reply. You cannot have the opportunity for reflection without an opportunity to delay and this is a tension with which we live in our online communities. Similarly, an IWB (computer plus interactive screen) enables the storage of large amounts of data in electronic format and hence affords an opportunity for teachers to prepare coherent, multimedia presentations before they go into the classroom. However, digital storage can also be a constraint in the classroom as teachers often prepare their lessons so diligently in advance that they 'over-present' (or talk for too long) and become less spontaneous in their classroom interaction. Thus, it is important not to see tools as unequivocally good, but to look for a mix of opportunity and constraint within them and try to work through these tensions in practice.

A final aspect of Gibson's concept of affordance, which has not had the attention it deserves, is the idea of direct perception. Gibson is interested in the immediate association we make with an object, in other words we jump to all sorts of spontaneous judgements about the use of a tool or artefact without being aware of our chain of thought. For example, we do not ask ourselves whether a wall is climbable, we immediately perceive it as affording climbing (or not), say, if we are being chased by a large dog.

Direct perception may help in understanding differentiated take-up of technology. As an example, I spent some years introducing students to the programming language Logo. These were beginner teachers interested in technology as a subject in the school and they made a receptive audience. However, reactions to Logo varied. Each year I taught it, around a third of students saw Logo as immediately playful and inherently interesting. They were quickly engaged in solving some problems I had given them and got on with designing their own ideas for classroom teaching. If Logo was present in the schools in which they were going to teach they would feel prepared to use it and would happily get on with. Around a third had their doubts; Logo was not designed with ease of use in mind and it was making complicated what was really more straightforward to do in other ways. These student teachers would use Logo in school if asked but they would not lead on it. A final third struggled to see its application at all, seeing it as a poor example of a design package. I found these experiences enlightening for the variety of associations made with the technology but also noticed the durability of their attitudes as I came to visit them in schools over the year. Of course, in-service and pre-service classes aim to help prospective teachers think through their responses to technology and provide a reasoned basis for future practice, but once an immediate association was made with technology, in this case Logo, it could be very difficult to shift.

We live in hybrid environments

Participation with technology was and still is often thought of in binary terms, we are either online or offline, but this is not right: we are increasingly online and offline at the same time (for example, de Souza e Silva, 2006; Eyal and Gil, 2022). We gain our sense of community and belonging from those we meet online as much as from those we meet F2F.

Understanding hybridity is important when it comes to education and particularly important when it comes to remote learning. Eyal and Gil describe how the experience of conducting live classes during the COVID-19 lockdown sensitised them to the context in which students learnt in ways they had not fully appreciated before. This was a common experience. In my own online teaching I could see students who were hampered by faltering internet connections and some who were interrupted by children coming in and out of the room. Students could be seen in cars, en route to other places, sitting in airport lounges or in bedrooms in quarantine or self-isolation accommodation. Learners would access classes within different time zones, some looking tired and ready for bed, others had just got up. This was an eye-opener. Of course, I had always understood that contexts differ but I had become used to producing learning material, putting it online and letting it go. Faced with the reality of live classes, I could see how important time and place were when learning at a distance. The idea that online learning was anywhere, anytime went out of the window, it was taking place at a very definite time and place and in many cases being fitted in around difficult constraints.

Understanding the hybrid nature of digital technology suggest that terms such as 'virtual participation', 'cyberspace' and 'online presence' are suspect as they suggest that we have in some way left our bodies behind when online, when this is not the case at all (see Wilson et al, 2017). For example, in one early account, Lindtner et al (2008) observed online gamers in China in their favourite play locations, including internet cafes (or *wang ba*) and student dormitories. The researchers were interested in how participation in online games was shaped by the contexts in which playing took place. For example, rather than play alone, as might be assumed was normal practice, gamers would deliberately sit next to other players in their favourite *wang ba* in order to discuss what they were doing. Some contrasted the more stimulating experience of playing in the presence of others with the flatter experience of playing alone at home. Participants also talked about how gaming had become the subject of a wider discourse in the media, gaining attention from the authorities, and this had affected their feelings about their pastime. For Lindtner et al (2008), online activity is a 'kind of assemblage' of objects, people and technologies rather than something happening in a far-off cyberspace.

How might educators react to hybridity? One approach has been to continue to think in terms of binary spaces and make sure that learners get access to both physical and online experiences. Thus, blended learning has the idea of mixing, in various combinations, web-supported resources with F2F teaching. This has practical application in the idea of the flipped classroom (see Akçayır and Akçayır, 2018). But, more radically, we can think of hybridity as a blurring or merging of spaces. One example of this is the reconceptualisation of the library as a learning space in which learners have access to physical books but also access to eBooks and other resources so that library staff become 'information specialist, instructional partner, and technology ally' (Subramaniam et al, 2012). Extending this approach, institutions, particularly in higher education, have made the idea of a learning space or 'learning grid' popular – a space in which learners can meet physically but have easy access to IWB and the internet. Some writers are now further promoting the concept of the 'Internet of Things' in the classroom and this raises the profile of tools such as readers, scanners, voice recognition and other devices to facilitate teaching (for example, Kassab et al, 2020). However, the most obvious aspect of hybridity does not concern what institutions provide for learners, but what the learners carry about with them and that is often the mobile phone. As seen earlier, this has generated the concept of mobile learning, one important application of which has been the provision of materials and support for professional learning outside of the classroom (for example, Clay, 2011). With mobile technology, the classroom itself can become increasingly hybrid. For example, in a language classroom students access online dictionaries to avoid disrupting the lesson with their questions, rehearse what they want to say in the target language with the help of translation software, and enter new words to vocabulary training programmes in situ. Further, teachers in many classrooms in which an IWB is missing might use WhatsApp or other group lists on their mobile phone to share presentations with students in the classroom itself. Of course, many teachers have an understandable reluctance to allow mobile devices in the classroom and there can be a mismatch between students' use of mobile devices and their productive use in the classroom, but their potential value in a hybrid version of learning is not in doubt.

We participate in assemblages of people and objects

An offshoot in the discussion of hybridity takes us into the language of assemblage, of actor network theory (ANT) and related theories that come under the banner of science and technology studies (STS). These approaches are as interested in non-digital as well as digital artefacts and one classic study concerns the design of a bicycle (Bijker, 1997). This study was an eye-opener at the time for it showed that successful innovations were not about the superiority of a new technology but to what degree changes were found acceptable by 'relevant social groups'. In the case of the bicycle, we might think that innovative design was all about speed and efficiency but for some groups comfort might have been a more important factor, and for others adventure, not speed, was what was required. Thus designs become established through a process of negotiation until they become settled.

Bijker went further than to suggest that social groups saw artefacts in different ways – they wanted to show how an artefact was an expression of users' preference in the first place. This is not an easy idea but in terms of digital technology an example might be the relationship many Apple Mac users had with their machines. It was not simply that they wanted to use 'a computer', but they wanted to use one that they felt had embedded the values of creativity into its design. In other words, they had, or at least felt they had, jointly created the artefact. This is the idea of *enrolment* in that both human (Apple users) and non–human actors (Apple computers) become assembled together in a system of technology use. These kinds of assemblages spring up all over the place, say, in open-source, girl gaming, cool PC users communities and so on. ANT is particularly useful for showing that assemblages have the appearance of being stable but they need to be worked on – in the case of computers through user groups, influencers on social networking sites, specialist support services, retail outlets and so on. However, networks can quickly dissolve and reconstitute themselves elsewhere as the short history of social networking attest. A strength of ANT is a 'principle of symmetry' requiring an even-handed analysis of winners and losers when it comes to design and an encouragement to think how outcomes could have been different.

One example of using ANT as a theoretical frame is Colton (2019) looking at challenge-based learning among young learners in Australia. Colton uses ANT to frame her observations of the classroom around a coming together of materials and people and practices. In the study material elements included 'laptops, wi-fi, break out space, furniture and multimedia presentations' (Colton, 2019: 427) and these were as important as the people (and their related discourses) with which these materials interacted. The study reported on a practice of 'break-out learning' which was 'open, free and unbounded' and a performance in which students were 'seen to direct their own learning as they managed their own movements and activities, albeit in a way which was delineated by institutional rules and practices that restricted movement' (Colton, 2019: 429). Break-out learning then had as much to do with artefacts and environment as it did with teachers and their perspectives on teaching. Case 5.2 presents a further example, taken from higher education.

Case 5.2: The role of professional identity in patterns of use of multiple-choice assessment tools (Johannesen and Habib, 2010)

What is this about?

The paper is focused on the use of VLEs in a higher education institution in Norway. The authors are interested in how university lecturers used the VLE and looked specifically at how different departments responded to the opportunity to create multiple-choice tests. They wanted to explore how decisions about the use of the multiple-choice tool were influenced by professional roles and identities. To do this, they carried out a case study in the faculties of nursing, teacher education and engineering. Their study involved F2F interviews and personal logs (diaries) kept by the participants, with details of their VLE-based activities.

What did they find?

They found attitudes and practice towards online multiple-choice assessment tools varied across the three faculties. In engineering, in spite of some expressed scepticism, multiple-choice tests were used and considered to be an appropriate assessment method. In education, multiple-choice tests were seen as incompatible with the idea of learning embraced in the faculty, and tended not to be used at all. The third faculty, nursing, was in many ways the most interesting as staff found that students had created their own multiple-choice questions for each other using the software. Aware of the popularity of this practice, staff created an assessment task which involved working in small groups to develop a multiple-choice test and subsequently submit the test to their fellow students.

What theoretical frameworks influenced their research?

The researchers were influenced by community of practice theory and in particular the idea that identity was 'a negotiated experience of the self'. In other words one's sense of self was formed and expressed within the communities in which one participated. A second influential theory in this study was ANT, with its idea that humans and non-humans may be considered actors creating networks of practice. A key facet of ANT is the multidimensional nature of technology, people see different values in tools and try to define tool use in a certain way. This means that users do not always see a tool in the way that designers intend. Indeed, in this study teachers within the faculties of engineering and education saw multiple-choice software as an assessment tool and had competing perspectives on the value of such assessment. Neither faculty had considered the students creating their own tests. In contrast, teachers in the nursing faculty had created a novel assessment exercise based around group collaboration. By combining an interest in CoP with an interest in ANT the authors felt they could not only focus on the different ways people saw a tool but how their perspectives were shaped by the community. It was a study of people + tools + community.

What does this say about theorising technology?

The paper shows the value of flexibility, this would have been a lesser study if only about CoP or about ANT. By combining theoretical frameworks the authors were able to offer a more insightful interpretation of, in this case, multiple-choice software. It also shows the value of researcher immersion in the environment in which technology is used.

What difficulties does the paper present?

By focusing on community the researchers may have underplayed the agency of individual lecturers. For example, could individual lecturers think about and use technology in a different way to the 'values embraced by the faculty'? And who was it who noticed that students were writing their own quizzes, and why did this take off as an assessment practice? It would have been interesting too if the researchers had traced the history of VLE design, for example, what did the designers intend when they included multiple-choice software? Finally, the paper shows that theoretical framing can inform practice but the implications are not spelt out. A reasonable conclusion, however, is not to be dogmatic about technology and to observe and listen to students as they may have interesting ways of transforming the use of tools.

The social shaping of technology

ANT has the considerable advantage of bringing material objects centre stage into the study of the use of technology but is often criticised for underplaying the ways in which social, economic and political relationships frame its use and create the conditions for an artefact to be produced in the first place. For example, if technocentrists see the steam engine as powering the industrial revolution, Marxists such as Hobsbawm (1999) note that the technology of steam power was long known and such a revolution in manufacturing could have happened much earlier; it was the legal, political and economic context that created the industrial revolution not the technology. Fast forward and today we have whole industries of people working to improve processing speeds of computers, create new software, expand the reach of the internet and so on, but these attempts only make sense in the context of market competition and the search for market dominance.

The social shaping of technology then suggests that while actors may be assembled there is someone else, or something else, pulling the strings. Taken to extremes the social shaping of technology offers a deterministic and perhaps depressing view of human endeavour: are we to write out the contribution of individuals in all attempts at technological innovation? Certainly not, but when we understand technology as shaped by social forces then we can see that innovation does not emerge out of thin air, it builds on what has been developed in the past and becomes used, or not used, depending on how it fits social structures. In other words, technology practices develop according to a wider sociological logic. One example of this is the way that computing, both in the home and school, has been influenced by wider assumptions around gender, so that it was seen as important in male socialisation but subsidiary in female (Clegg and Trayhurn, 2000; Clegg, 2001). Thus, it is not surprising that there was a gender imbalance in terms of those taking up computing in school and within the computer industry more widely. Gender, further, influenced the way that computing was taught and there are long-standing differentials too in who gets to access technology when it is a scarce resource in the school and in the home.

Social class plays an important role too in the shaping of technology and a study of access to mobile phones in Sri Lanka (Wijetunga, 2014; Case 5.3) shows that underprivileged youth did not see the same affordances in phone technology as the new urban middle class. Class played an important role too in remote learning during the COVID-19 pandemic lockdown. Continuation of learning was made difficult, often impossible, if families lacked money to buy computers, or at least a mobile phone, in order to access learning, but this problem was compounded by some children's lack of access to social and cultural capital. This meant that some children were isolated whereas others had access to large networks of support.

However social shaping of technology can extend beyond more obvious economic categories into questions of organisational culture. This was shown in Johannesen and Habib (2010), in that perceptions of multiple-choice software were shaped by departmental cultures. In a similar vein, Costa (2015) shows that the opportunities that technology provided for enhanced sharing between academics and the public, and the opening of an open access movement, were not fully realised as they ran up against established academic practices. These practices privileged articles in subscription journals, which were by default closed-access. As with Wijetunga, Costa discusses her findings in relation to Bourdieu's idea of habitus, or disposition within a field. This suggests that when we try to exercise agency and develop a new habitus, we come up against the constraints of taken-for-granted ways of behaving. There is a similar message in Johnson's (2019) study of mobile technology and young people. The tension here is that young people have a habitus (in the sense of learned habits, bodily skills and tastes that 'go without saying') when it comes to using mobile phones that is not aligned to contemporary schooling.

One further example of how technology is shaped lies in the choices over software in schools. In an obvious way it does not matter much who designed the software, any more than it matters who produced the pencils students write with or the paper that they write on. However, the character of the software does matter when it comes to looking at what gets into education and what does not. One historical example of this is the decline of 'small' programmes designed by teachers and developed within support centres in the earlier days of computing. Some of these programmes embedded a pedagogical principle that students had to understand what they wanted to do, as was the case with Logo discussed earlier, even if this made the programmes more convoluted. As the vocational rationale tended to dominate in respect to technology, software instead came to be chosen for its industry application, meaning that younger learners were using unsuitable software such as Excel, World and Access, designed for commercial settings. Moreover, these programmes were designed with ease of use in mind. This seems fine but it meant that students were put in the role of user and not learner and they could be led into carrying out actions which they did not understand. A consequence was that several programmes were eased out of schools even though they were designed with educational principles not commercial application in mind (see, for example, Ball, 1990).

Case 5.3: The digital divide objectified in the design: use of the mobile telephone by underprivileged youth in Sri Lanka (Wijetunga, 2014)

What is this about?

This is about the use of mobile phones among young people. The authors note that there was some optimism that the digital divide might be shrinking because of access to mobile phones among hard-to-reach communities in developing countries such as Sri Lanka in which this study took place. Thus, they investigated mobile phone use among two groups of users aged 19–25 years. One group represented the socioeconomic elite of the society ('new urban middle class' or UMC) and the second group represented a lower socioeconomic stratum, those employed in semi- or unskilled manual work and coming from rural regions of the country. Participants in this group had received no higher education and were classified as 'underprivileged youth' (UY).

Mobile phone use was widespread for all youth in the study and important to their identity. Even though faced with financial constraints, the UY actively pursued similar handsets to the UMC. However, there were clear differences in how they used these phones so that they generally stuck to the most basic functions, for the most part talk and text. They did not routinely access social networks or load and download pictures or generally browse the internet.

Why this differentiated use?

Reasons included language (instructions were in English, a language in which UY had minimum proficiency) and lack of previous exposure to smart phones. In contrast, computing and internet browsing were familiar activities for UMC and were perceived as affordances of phones in ways in which they were not for UY. UY lacked the cultural and social capital to make full use of the phones, UMC did not. This means that even when the ICTs finally become affordable, they cannot be effectively used because the designs presuppose users who possess the necessary cultural capital.

What is good about this paper?

The account offers a convincing explanation of the phenomenon of differentiated use and does this by presenting a more holistic picture than in many other studies. Inequalities are often discussed in terms of physical access to devices but this paper shows the importance of cultural and social capital too. As with Johannesen and Habib (2010), Wijetunga usefully merges different conceptual tools – in this case he draws on Bourdieu, to understand social class, and Gibson, to understand affordances.

How do these findings transfer to education?

Very easily. We must consider much more than access to technology when introducing digital tools.

What difficulties does the paper present?

Perhaps the study underestimates not just the cost of the phone itself but the cost of contracts or pay-as-you-go plans. These costs could make, say, surfing the web impossible to afford. It would also be interesting to see how far their conceptualisation works to explain further use of mobile phones in Sri Lanka since the study was undertaken.

Is the important question: 'what ought technology to be?'

Many of the sociological approaches towards technology are understandably concentrating on how technology is used, but a more educational approach is to explore ways that technology *could be* used for more equitable and democratic purposes. This leads us to participatory approaches to design, for example research-based design, co-design, co-creation, user and learner-centred design, plus a distinctive design thinking approach. All of these require the direct and early involvement of 'stakeholders' to produce designs which are usable – though who the stakeholders are and how great their involvement needs to be debated. Participatory approaches work best when the designer is faced with so-called 'wicked' problems for which there are no obvious solutions, and in contexts in which there are many competing voices. Participatory approaches frequently run up against the instrumental concerns of more conventional design methodology ('How can we meet the design brief as quickly and cost-effectively as possible?') and critics will see the intense involvement of stakeholders as time-consuming and hence expensive. They would much rather we just got on with it.

There is not space to consider all variants of participatory design but design thinking gives a feel (see Razzouk and Shute, 2012). Design thinking draws upon research in different fields though has had a long-standing association with the Hasso–Plattner Institute of Design at Stanford University. A shorthand model for the process is that of:

- Empathise – this involves observing and engaging with stakeholders to understand their practices and perspectives.
- Define – this involves drawing out the key aspects of the problem being addressed, it is important to express the problem in human-to-human rather than technical terms.
- Ideate – this is coming up with new ideas about solving the problem.
- Prototype – this is producing mock-ups/inexpensive prototypes so that that a solution can be better visualised by stakeholders.
- Test – this involves testing the most likely solution but with the understanding that the process may need to begin again if the innovation did not work as imagined.

As an approach it is similar to action research, discussed in Chapter 1, but it is specially tailored to the idea of artefact design, about which there are several studies. For example, Jadán-Guerrero et al (2020) discuss working with student teachers to address how hybrid tools could support young children, including children with special educational needs. The paper describes three prototypes: *interactive books*, combining traditional fairytale books with mobile devices, such as QR codes and near field communication tags to 'give life to the stories'; *educational board games* with augmented reality markers to help players; *tangible educational resources* which integrate Makey-Makey device (this allows everyday objects to connect to computer keys) and/or Scratch (a simple visual programming language) with everyday objects including fruit, clay and aluminium foil.

A further example of participatory design looks at how critical ICT engagement may be enhanced by visual methods in developing countries (or the global south). Bentley et al (2019) present three mini case studies.

The first takes place in a Brazilian *favela* (or 'shantytown') and involved Nemer working with local people to create a photograph book. This book contained 60 photos and short texts, which highlighted social issues around the use of technology. An important aim was to address stereotypical assumptions about life in *favelas* and to show how problems of access had not so much been overcome but worked around. Visual methods were used as they were more appropriate in a context in which many local people struggled with reading and writing.

The second case explored the user of ICT within Gender Links, a civil society organisation aimed at supporting greater gender equity at a local level in southern Africa. Bentley asked stakeholders to sketch, using pen and paper, how they saw ICT as contributing to resolving problems. Once participants had finished drawing, Bentley and the volunteer participants discussed the pictures to understand how stakeholders saw the role of ICT. This offered no easy solutions and Bentley notes a tension between her view of technology and that of her participants:

> From the modeling interviews, it was apparent that staff did not see any problems with the ways in which they used ICTs to learn from their beneficiaries, about organizational practice or to share knowledge with their donors, contrary to dominant discourses. However, I had observed staff overwhelmed at work, struggling to balance heavy workloads, and to respond effectively to their growing numbers of diverse beneficiaries. One officer drew a picture of himself atop an anvil with a hammer positioned over his head to convey the amount of pressure he felt daily. All other staff reflected on how the stressful work environment affected the quality of work, and their relationships with beneficiaries. Yet, staff did not view ICT as a means to resolve these problems. There was a disjoint between my perspective and theirs, as I could see many opportunities to use ICT to reduce workload pressure. Yet, I lacked the power and position to convince staff to pursue these options amidst their overwhelming schedules. Having the rich pictures to refer to during our discussions was important for establishing these differences, and to influence staff perceptions of these matters. (Bentley et al, 2019: 486)

A third example covered Community Multimedia Centres in Mozambique. Here Vannini used photos as part of an interview process (or photo-elicitation) to understand local stakeholders' understanding of technology and of public access facilities. Discussing the photos together led to ideas for improvement, and Vannini stresses the importance of enabling participants to contribute to the use or design of ICT.

Participatory practices in developing countries lead on to the idea of decolonising methodology. This is a broad term but implies an attempt is made to address imbalances in structural and cultural institutions. As regards ICT design, decolonising prioritises community representation within research teams and within research practices. It sees technology practices as having been framed through a global north lens and seeks to give back to the communities in appropriate ways. Perhaps the approach can be summed up by showing respect for indigenous perspectives (Lazem et al, 2021).

How then should we think about technology?

The value and shortcomings of the various perspectives are put forward in Table 5.1.

Table 5.1: Pros and cons of different perspectives on technology

Perspective	What is the big idea?	What value has it got?	What drawbacks are there?	Theoretical underpinning
Technocentric	Tools will be used in predictable ways across contexts; tools impact directly on social, political and economic life; technology will help alleviate educational problems	Focuses attention on the useful features of technology	Underplays the importance of context; a tool can be used in very many ways; can lead to unhelpful kinds of evaluation	Light on theoretical backing but may draw on learning theory or a version of affordances
Affordance	Tools have properties which afford actions; these properties can generate countless affordances; affordances need to be perceived	Captures the idea that technology is both an object and a perception; may help develop a more inquiring and exploratory view of technology	Is largely based on psychology of perception; does not itself provide an account of the social shaping of technology use	Gibson (1986)
Hybridity	Social participation takes place in merged online and offline worlds	Shows online activity to be embodied; context matters when looking at technology use	Can over-focus on micro world of the learners and miss the wider picture	Varied may draw on STS
Networks of users and technology	The world is created through assemblies of people, objects and discourse	Brings tools into the mainstream of social science; shows the varied perceptions and discourses around technology; accounts for both stability and disruption	The idea of non-human actor is challenging; tends to show that users have different perceptions of a tool rather than why they see these tools as they do	ANT (see Latour, Bilker and others). ANT is more an approach than a single theory
Social shaping	Tools are designed and used according to an underlying political/social/economic logic; class, gender and ethnicity are important when considering differentiated impact of technology	Shows that asymmetries in access to forms of capital distorts opportunities for different groups	Needs to be presented with subtlety and flexibility – use is shaped not determined by social factors; may underestimate the disruptive potential of the tool	Will draw on varied social theory, Bourdieu in particular
Action oriented	The goal is to shape technology use to need	Focused on practical application; respectful of local context	May be time-consuming; may be overly optimistic about the power to change practices	Participatory design theories, pragmatic action research, design thinking

The *technocentric* view is one in which technology can be described and its use predicted, at least up to a point. It can lead to a rose-tinted view of technology and a wish list of functions. Its theoretical underpinning is weak but much stronger when linked with learning theories through the involvement of subject experts. Often those writing about technology can be seen as technocentric but they may simply be putting forward their own ideas on how technology could be used. *Affordances* were introduced as a way of unsettling the idea of technology use was 'invariant' by drawing attention to the varied nature of perception: the same artefact can be seen in many different ways. Affordance is a psychological rather than a sociological concept and has less to offer in understanding the wider context in which technology is used.

The idea of *hybridity*, that is, the mixing of physical and online participation, is liberating as it brings technology use 'back to earth' and punctures the idea that being online is the same as being disembodied. This has important considerations for education both in F2F and distance and remote learning. It also leads to understanding that there are *networks of users and technology*. Here ANT makes an important contribution. Previous approaches have focused on perception of technology but in ANT the technology is itself an actant and forms part of a network or assemblage of practice. However, ANT may be much better at explaining how assemblages come about rather than the social forces which lead them to come about. This gap is addressed in the *social shaping of the technology* which shows that technology is shaped, and often distorted, through asymmetries in social and cultural worlds. Addressing these asymmetries forms part of the *action-oriented approach* to design in which users are expected to empathise and engage with stakeholders in a democratic spirit.

Underlying all these different perspectives on technology are important questions such as 'Is technology a thing that we can take control of and use for our own purposes?', 'Is it something which is shaped by existing social institutions?', 'Does it have an animacy of its own?'.

Summary

This chapter has taken us through ways of theorising technology and I have:

- shown that there are radically different ways of understanding technology;
- described technocentric views as taking technology as 'invariant' and use as predictable;
- explained the importance of researching physical settings, resulting in hybrid views of technology;
- seen assemblage as an 'enrolling' of objects, technology and people;
- looked at how social and economic structures shape the design and use of technology; and

- suggested that each perspective on technology comes with pros and cons and that some propose action-oriented, or participatory, approaches to the design of technology.

Where to read more

The case studies cited in the chapter are all accessible and clearly illustrate different perspectives on technology. In regard to affordances, more can be found on realist and subjectivist philosophy in Turvey (1992). On ANT I found Prout (1996) a helpful introduction and Wilson et al (2017) an alternative take on assemblage to ANT, using learning analytics as a case. MacKenzie and Wajcman (1999) provide a helpful discussion of the social shaping of technology and a wider introduction to STS. As seen in the chapter Bourdieu is an important point of reference when it comes to technology use and his original elaboration of three forms of capital is set out in Bourdieu (1986). Grenfell's (2004) gives a readable introduction to his work.

Those looking for a more philosophical view of technology, might try the edited book by Shrader-Frechette and Westra (1997).

6

Optimism and pessimism when it comes to theorising technology

I have looked at theorising learners and learning, teachers and teaching, and finally technology itself in the previous three chapters and I can now step back to consider a wider theme: how far should we see technology, including its impact on education, in positive or negative terms? This represents a change of perspective. This is looking at wider narratives about technology, not just at theories developed within academia. This is important as what we think about technology is heavily influenced by a wider discourse and in this chapter I present two starkly different kinds of narratives. I go on to then suggest that a more balanced approach is possible. I cover:

• Optimistic accounts of technology
• Pessimism about technology
• Comparing optimistic and pessimistic perspectives

Optimistic accounts of technology

The optimistic view is informed by the idea that technology has enabled fantastic scientific and cultural achievements and made us who we are today. Our history as a species is an uninterrupted line of technological development, going right back to the invention of neolithic stone tools. This idea is captured in iconic form in Kubrick's film *2001: A Space Odyssey*. The film famously begins with an anthropoid monkey that picks up an animal bone, and realises this can be transformed into a tool, in the story the bone becomes a club. With tools begins language and with tools plus language everything is possible. To stress the point, the film fast forwards to a space station of the future; from a simple realisation that artefacts can become tools we end up being able to traverse the universe.

For the optimist, technology makes our lives longer, more comfortable, more varied, more interesting. Tools can be used destructively for sure, but optimists stress our ability to tame baser instincts and channel tool use into creative and unselfish ends. This is captured powerfully in the advertising of digital tools. Apple in the 1980s managed to re-invent personal computing from something geeky or business oriented into something cool. In time Microsoft followed: 'Where do you want to go today?' asked Microsoft in a famous 2004 advertisement and the answer was that with technology you could go anywhere you wanted.

Optimists point to the speed with which digital technology is advancing. Only a few years ago computer professionals debated at length whether it would be ever possible for a computer to play chess given the vast, in practical terms infinite, number of moves that are possible during a game (Jackson, 2019). Now with a combination of pattern recognition, rapid processing and enhanced data storage a computer program can beat any person on Earth. Likewise, a machine for carrying out rapid translation of text was fantastical – the thing of science fiction – but neural machine translation will provide a workable translation of many different languages using a standard personal computer. It is a cliché, but nonetheless still startling, that we now have within our mobile devices access to many times more computing power than that used to land a man on the moon (Kendall, 2019).

Optimists are aware of counter-narratives. For example, personal access to digital tools was seen as leading to a breakdown of the family and atomisation of society, but the opposite they claim has happened. Social networks have helped provide the loose ties that bind society together. An early proponent of this view was the community network pioneer Rheingold (1993) who argued that on-screen interaction was every bit as varied as offline but also with far wider reach:

> People in virtual communities use words on screen to exchange pleasantries and argue, engage in intellectual discourse, conduct commerce, exchange knowledge, share emotional support, make plans, brainstorm, gossip, feud, fall in love, find friends and lose them, play games, flirt, create a little high art and a lot of idle talk. People in virtual communities do just about everything people do in real life, but we leave our bodies behind. You can't kiss anybody and nobody can punch you on the nose, but a lot can happen within these boundaries. To the millions have who have been drawn into it, the richness and vitality of computer linked cultures is attractive, even addictive. There is no such thing as a single, monolithic, online subculture; it's more like an ecosystem of subcultures, some frivolous, others serious. The cutting edge of scientific discourse is migrating to virtual communities, where you can read the electronic pre-pre-printed reports of molecular biologists and cognitive scientists. At the same time, activists and educational reformers are using the same medium as a political tool. You can use virtual communities to find a date, sell a lawnmower, publish a novel, conduct a meeting. (Rheingold, 1993: 3)

The internet has enabled a web of networks at work, family and social life to flourish. For optimists, our post-industrial society, or new information age, looks a lot like the one futurologists such as Toffler (1980) predicted: a shift from mass consumption, mass education, mass media towards a society characterised by 'flexibility, pluralism, humanised technology and ecological sensitivity'. This networking has been particularly helpful for young people by facilitating their capacity to connect and generate a spirit of community mindedness. Online spaces are sites for discovering 'versions of the self' and help adolescents gain a sense of identity and ownership (boyd, 2014). An example here is Cole et al (2011) who discuss the evolution of 'Gimpgirl' which began as collaboration of young women with disabilities who wanted to create a safe and informal online space for sharing ideas and experiences, and for offering information and peer-to-peer support. The community evolved as it adapted to ever changing software (listservs, interactive virtual worlds, websites, blogs and various social networks) but always maintained a sense of inclusion. Online worlds can be playful, too. Thomas (2005) explored the online activities of a group of children interested in Tolkien's world of Middle Earth and found they engaged in online role-playing and used avatars for poetry recitals and storytelling.

When it comes to formal education, progress with technology has been slower than optimists would like. However it has made its mark. Consider reach. Postal services allowed for correspondence courses so that learners at a distance could access tutors by mail. In time packages of printed course materials, videos and tape recordings could also be sent. Television and radio next came to be used to support open universities and open education in initiatives such as India's National Open School and Telesecundaria in Mexico. With internet technology television could be replaced with 'live classes', something particularly important in China as a means of addressing unequal opportunities in rural areas (McQuiade, 2009). The idea was that learners could access presentations made by skilled teachers online when before these were only accessible to those in more elite city schools or universities. This system was sometimes known as the 'two-teacher' classroom, hinting at the opportunities of having a local teacher mediate the content before, during or after the presentation.

Crossing distance has been very important not just for disadvantaged communities but became a major issue during the lockdown of schools and other institutions related to the COVID-19 pandemic; technology enabled education to continue remotely. A lot of the emphasis was on online classes (for example, Xue et al, 2020) and MOOCs came into their own as accessible learning platforms for adult learners but also for younger learners in unplanned ways. However, this was not one-size-fits-all and optimists point to the ability of governments to offer a pragmatic mix of technology-based solutions reflecting national settings. These solutions included educational television and radio as well as national platforms of virtual learning and e-libraries (Pradhan and Hyde, 2022). In many cases, mobile phones rather than computers played an important role in facilitating access, particularly in developing countries.

Low and high technology solutions are needed as access remains an issue, not just access to the internet but in many countries access to electricity supply in the first place. But here again optimists can see successes. They point not only to large-scale partnerships between governments and international partners to expand the reach of technology but also to small-scale and more flexible innovations. An example of this is the 'School in a Bag' (SMART, nd). The 'Bag' is delivered by motorbike or even on foot, and initially included a laptop, smart phone, LED television, five tablet machines, hard drive with educational content and pocket Wi-Fi, with later packages including a projector, teacher laptop and DVD player. The lack of electricity is addressed by including a solar panel to charge devices. Initiatives like these cannot address wider development issues but they are important ways of providing hard-to-reach communities with educational resources.

Technology does not stand still. At the time of writing there is excitement about the application of artificial intelligence (AI) and robotics for education, which in the words of one paper has 'innovated teaching methods, enriched instructional tools, changed learning environments, redefined the roles of teachers and students and constructed a new type of educational ecology' (Yueh and Chiang, 2020: 1804). These are early days but children can already learn with robots using natural language. In one study a humanoid robot, 'Julia', conversed and provided support for children's reading, seeming to display patience and empathy and proving popular with children (Yueh and Chiang, 2020). Similar AI 'chatbots' have provided opportunities for improving language learners' communicative competence. We do not know where all this will lead but optimists see order arising out of a free exchange of ideas; the best applications will rise to the top.

One reason underlying the optimists' position is that young people are excited about technology. Turkle's (2005 [first edition 1984]) study explored young people's enthusiasm for computers. She described their relationship to machines in almost metaphysical terms: the computer is something young people want to feel mastery over and see their own competence as important to their sense of identity. These were early days but Turkle set a trend of observing and valuing what young people were doing with computers, looking at who, in Rogers's words, we could call innovators and early adopters. In a similar vein, Gee (2018) looked at online networks and noted that much more was going on in terms of cognitive and social skills development in playing online games than critics realised. Gee, as seen in Chapter 3, drew attention to the importance of affinity spaces for young people. The celebratory tone of reporting was accentuated by Prensky (2001: 2), who argued that contemporary students were the first generation to grow up with computer technology: 'Today's average college grads have spent less than 5,000 hours of their lives reading, but over 10,000 hours playing video games (not to mention 20,000 hours watching TV). Computer games, email, the Internet, cell phones and instant messaging are integral parts of their lives.' He argued – and more or less took it as read – that these online experiences meant that students think and process information in a fundamentally different way. Technology exposure had for Prensky, as it had for Siemens, literally re-structured young people's brains. This goes too far, but the least one can say is that their thinking patterns have changed. For Prensky the biggest problem facing education at the time was that adult instructors (so-called digital immigrants) were left struggling to teach a population which worked in a different way. In contrast to how learning took place in school, digital natives were:

> used to receiving information really fast. They like to parallel process and multi-task. They prefer their graphics before their text rather than the opposite. They prefer random access (like hypertext). They function best when networked. They thrive on instant gratification and frequent rewards. They prefer games to 'serious' work. They have little patience for lectures, step-by-step logic, and 'tell-test' instruction. (Prensky, 2001: 1)

Perhaps Prensky's case is overblown, but there are more subtle arguments for change as well. For example, the new literacies movement celebrated young people's agency in digital spaces (for example, Leu et al, 2004) and noted that reading today embraces much more than printed text. Teachers need to understand how young people use language when they engage with gaming software, internet search engines, social media and so on, not just how they engage with physical books.

Any discussion of literacy has to take in information literacy so that students are introduced to an information handling cycle of asking questions and then 'locate information, critically evaluate the usefulness of that information, synthesize information to answer those questions, and then communicate the answers to others' (Leu et al, 2004: 1572). Information processing is so important to contemporary education as it is a skill needed not just for social but for workplace participation. The Organisation for Economic Co-operation and Development (OECD) noted that in the new knowledge economies memorisation of facts and procedures was not enough for success:

> Educated workers need a conceptual understanding of complex concepts, and the ability to work with them creatively to generate new ideas, new theories, new products, and new knowledge. They need to be able critically to evaluate what they read, be able to express themselves clearly both verbally and in writing, and understand scientific and mathematical

thinking. They need to learn integrated and usable knowledge, rather than the sets of compartmentalised and de-contextualised facts. They need to be able to take responsibility for their own continuing, life-long learning. Students must be able to use technology to learn content and skills – so that they know how to learn, think critically, solve problems, use information, communicate, innovate and collaborate. (Centre for Education Research and Innovation, 2008: 1)

The OECD (2017) later established principles for innovative learning and argued for the concept of 'learning environments' rather than 'schools' or 'classrooms', directing attention to both formal and informal kinds of learning. This call has been taken up. For example, Mogas et al (2022), as we saw in Chapter 1, explored the future of education within the 'fourth industrial revolution' (the digital revolution) and argued for aligning technology with more personalised systems of education. New 'smart' schools must be inclusive, sustainable and adopt new learning methodologies.

Fullan and Langworthy (2013), too, argued for curriculum change. Schools need to showcase competences such as critical thinking, creativity, communication and collaboration, rather than traditional subject teaching. This would better prepare young people for life-long learning but, not only that, it would engage their interest. Fullan and Langworthy note dryly that:

> [S]tudents are increasingly bored in school and ever more so as they go from grade to grade. ... For teachers one could say that there's only one thing worse than being bored and that is 'having to teach the bored.' Because students are bored, teachers are bored too and the system is 'pushing' students and teachers out of school. (Fullan and Langworthy, 2013: 23)

A problem for optimists is that it is difficult to stay optimistic about the impact of technology on formal education when there is too little evidence of change. This has led some writers to see the self-organising capacity of learners as a way of getting round inertia in the system. Self-organising harks back to a celebrated book written by Illich (1973), which argued for deschooling society; institutions were not needed, or at least not beyond a certain point, as learners could exchange expertise among themselves through 'skill exchanges', using circulated lists of people's skills, their availability, and where they could be reached. This was pre-internet and relied on paper print-outs but in more recent literature the idea of 'chaotic learning' using the internet has been promoted. As we saw in Chapter 3, Siemens (Case 3.1) believed that learning was not ordered or predictable but could be self-organised using technology mediated networks. A similarly upbeat argument case for technology was put by Mitra et al (2016) – this is reported later in more detail as Case 6.1 – who found that children could learn to use 'hole in the wall' computers for useful purposes. Neither Siemens nor Mitra entirely ruled out teacher or teaching mediation but such mediation was not a necessary condition for learning.

But perhaps optimists need not be disappointed about the take-up of technology in formal institutions if we look instead at what learners in these institutions are doing. Children are learning with technology even before they get to school and as they grow older they turn naturally to internet sources and networks to support their learning. With mobile technology adult learners are able to access 'anywhere anytime' learning, and trainee teachers, nurses, midwives, computer specialist and other professionals are able to find emotional and practical support from their peers, and able to access vocational guidance when and where they need it (for example, Clay, 2011).

Not all optimists need to be 'gung ho' about self-organised learning and promote instead more incremental and sustainable ICT development in schools. A report by NESTA (an innovation foundation based in UK) found impactful innovations and projects using technology in schools in Europe as well as in New Zealand and Brazil (Baker et al, 2019). Rather than showcase ground-breaking state of the art technology, or schools turned upside down, the report focused on showing small changes through the reorganisation of classrooms, providing reliable internet connections, and creating supportive, collaborative staff development. They looked in particular at four factors which could support such change:

- Scale: innovations should impact on several schools not just single schools working in isolation.
- Teachers: teachers should feel empowered.
- Context: changes should reflect the local context.
- Complexity: innovations should involve a wide range of actors.

This is just one report on how to bring about innovation but it lies in a tradition of school reform discussed in Chapter 4 stressing the importance of leading change in ecologically joined up ways. Change is possible.

Case 6.1: Learning at the edge of chaos: self-organising systems in education (Mitra et al, 2016)

What is this about?

The authors begin by noticing how schools have struggled to cope with change, in particular the growing use of technology. They suggest that this struggle was inevitable given that 'they (educational systems) assumed that learning required a teacher, a classroom of 36 square metres, 30 children, and classes lasting one hour: a model inherited from the oral tradition of 5,000 years ago ... they assumed a top-down, hierarchical, predictable and controllable world that progresses slowly'. Schools could not easily adapt to the idea that learning was no longer 'ordered, and controllable, and had become chaotic and probabilistic'.

In this contribution the authors reflect on a project known as 'hole in the wall' computing. Here, computers, connected to the internet, were embedded into walls in villages and urban slums in India. Children were given no instructions alongside the machines but were invited to try them out and see what they found. (The name 'hole in the wall' was previously used to describe self-access cashpoints and the computers look much like these cashpoints, though their screens were larger and placed at a convenient height for children to use.)

At the time of the study many children in India did not know what a computer was, but over time Mitra and his colleagues found that they could learn to use the computers to play games, download media, search for information and so on. Children did this outside of school and with no teacher input, moreover local adults knew nothing about how to use computers either. Children invariably worked in groups, interacting constantly with each other, in a somewhat chaotic way. Mitra and colleagues concluded that the children had learned to use the computers by themselves and had achieved learning outcomes unexpected for their age. This led them to suspect that 'their learning was the outcome of a self-organising system, in much the same way it is understood in the physical sciences or mathematics: a set of interconnected parts, each unpredictable, producing spontaneous order in an apparently chaotic situation'.

Although the study shows the value of self-organising systems, the authors noticed that support was useful and looked for volunteer teachers. Their suggested approach was known as the 'grandmother's method', a role that included standing behind the children, admiring their work, acting fascinated and praising them as much as possible. These experiences led them to try to expand Self-Organised Learning Environments into regular classrooms, community centres, specially designed labs and home-schooling. For each session, the teacher could provide the class with a challenging question. Children then worked in flexible groups and at the end of the session each group presented their findings to the rest of the class.

What is useful in this account?

It is an optimistic account of technology use in contexts in which access to learning is poorly developed. It is a practical innovation and appears to have had impact. It provides more support for exploratory, collaborative or problem-based learning (see Garrison et al, 2001; Scardamalia and Bereiter, 2006; Colton, 2019). The study is a helpful counterweight to the idea, or at least the crudely interpreted idea, of digital nativism.

These children did not know how to use computers and then they did. Age had nothing to do with it, it was experience that mattered.

What problems does it throw up?

It does not provide the detail of how children learn in self-organising systems: What kind of interactions worked? What stopped children getting side-tracked, and did it matter if they were? How did they ensure that groups were not dominated by individuals with the loudest voices? Were some children acting as a teacher presence as they become more skilled than others, both in terms of content knowledge and ICT skills?

Pessimism about technology

I turn now to a pessimistic view of technology and the first thing pessimists notice when it comes to discourse about technology, not just in education but in society in general, is that the reality rarely lives up to the promise. For example, computers were supposed to be taking the drudgery out of work and would release time for more leisure and cultural activity. This, alas, did not happen (Robins and Webster, 1988). Calculating working hours is not an exact business, but the evidence points to a marked decline in the working week over the course of the 20th century only for that decline to stall in the most recent years. In many developing countries working hours have not declined at all (Giattino et al, 2020). Worse, in the new information age, work was supposed to be characterised by life-long learning, collaborative teams and flattened hierarchies. However, for many people work is more intensive now than ever and the flexibility which online working offers is accompanied by greater surveillance and a sense of anxiety when not online. When it comes to manufacturing, production is still often organised around an extreme division of labour and a 'scientific organisation of production' as reports of the conditions under which digital tools such as computers and mobile phones are produced testify (for example, Altenried, 2020). Meanwhile, throughout the world, there is increasing criticism of the 'uberisation of jobs', in other words jobs carried out by independent contractors using digital platforms. Employers often offer 'zero hours' contracts and workers have lost the benefits which unionised labour gained (Dablanc et al, 2017). As consumers we are complicit and comprised. Tech companies collect vast amounts of data about us, often data which has no direct relevance for the ostensible purpose of the apps we are using. However these data can be sold to create profiles to fine-tune advertising and to shepherd users into echo chambers of like-minded thinking. The business of technological disruption is surveillance capitalism

(Zuboff, 2019); this is undermining social trust, social cohesion and family bonding on an unprecedented scale.

The intense engagement of young people with technology, presented as an asset by enthusiasts, becomes a further liability to pessimists. There is something nasty and addictive about the internet and young people are routinely exposed to inappropriate sexuality, the promotion of self-harm and other threats to health and well-being. For example, Mei et al (2022) report widespread psychological, physical and sleep problems caused by excessive mobile phone use in China and Bhagat et al (2020) similarly see a hunger for social online interaction as a factor in internet addiction. Greenfield (2015) earlier argued that instant access to information and networks, and to 'vivid virtual experiences', meant that online engagement was 'out-competing the dreary reality' of life:

> If you place a human brain, with its evolutionary mandate to adapt to its environment, in an environment where there is no obvious linear sequence, where facts can be accessed at random, where everything is reversible, where the gap between stimulus and response is minimal, and above all where time is short, then your train of thought could be derailed. Add in the sensory distractions of an all-encompassing and vivid audio-visual universe encouraging shorter spans for sustained attention, and you might become, as it were, a computer yourself: a system responding efficiently and processing information very well but devoid of deeper thought. (Greenfield, 2015: 12)

Rather than write about the 'hard wiring' of brains as in Prensky, Greenfield sees the mind as built to respond with 'exquisite sensitivity' to external influences and for more and more people those external influences include the screen. It might be that moderation is the key to healthy online participation but digital technology is so compelling that its use is difficult to control. We are not 'mastering technology', technology is exerting its power over us.

Further objections to the way we use technology

These reported concerns about screen life have been often expressed by those working within psychology and sometimes, as with Greenfield, from neuroscience. However, technology itself is critiqued from other, quite contrasting, directions. Three of these have roots in Critical Theory, progressivism and conservatism. A fourth objection is more pragmatic: the lack of impact.

Critical Theory was associated with the Frankfurt school, rooted in 1930s Germany. However, it became a source of inspiration for counter-cultural movements in western countries in the 1960s and has come in and out of fashion ever since. Through the work of Marcuse (for example, Marcuse, 2013/1964), Critical Theory came to take on an anti-technological association, notwithstanding that other critical theorists such as Heidegger and Habermas had different views. Marcuse's proposition was that people were being manipulated by machines, meaning our lives were characterised by alienation and distress. But how did technology do this to us? The answer was that decisions and actions which should be contested were taken for granted on grounds of efficiency. True rationality should consider ends, not just means, and values such as democracy and equity were getting squeezed out whenever technology was being used.

In its broader application Critical Theory is about subjecting all practice to criticism and saying how things could be better (Feenberg, 2017). In respect to digital tools in education this means asking who is promoting what and why: Who has a vested interest in technology use? (Answer: Large online learning publishers); What kind of surveillance is being carried out? (Answer: A lot that is hidden); Is technology being promoted for instrumental reasons rather than for the quality of the educational experience? (Answer: Yes, technology is evaluated for its impact on learning rather than on the quality of learning).

A second line of attack on technology, particularly its use with very young learners, comes from *progressivism*. This is surprising as progressive educators seem to have a lot in common with the educational reformers such as Fullan and Langworthy, as both seem to want children to have the freedom to explore and do away with stuffy instructional drill and practice teaching, rigid subject boundaries and children sitting in rows. However, writers in the progressive tradition – this is a tradition that goes back to Fröbel (1782–1852), Pestalozzi (1746–1827) and later Montessori (1870–1952) – wanted children to experience the natural world, and to entrust education to what some called the eternal powers of nature. This makes modern-day heirs to the progressive tradition worried about the substitution of direct experience of nature with proxy, technology mediated experience. They see dangers to children in the constant exposure to screens and the impact of violent or sexualised television, music and advertising (Elkin, 2007). Above all they lament the squeezing out of physical play. The problem again is the addictive potential of technology but this is coupled with a questioning of technology mediated experience in the first place.

From a rather different angle the reform of the curriculum has also been questioned by *conservatives* who argue for a core curriculum, held within strong subject boundaries, taught by instructional teachers. Writers in this tradition argue that there is a gap between teacher and child in terms of experience and knowledge and this was one reason why we had teachers and schools in the first place (see Arendt, 1961). Teachers need to show children principles and concepts which went beyond what they could glean for themselves through direct experience. Schools were not there to reflect society; they were repositories of knowledge that had been handed down over time. There is little in conservative writing that needs to disqualify the use of technology as a point of principle, for example the kind of practice software discussed by Banerjee et al (2007) and the introduction of IWBs could be seen as acceptable supports for instructional teaching. However, conservatives would have little sympathy for the kind of exploratory or problem-solving curriculum, discussed by Scardamalia and Bereiter (2006) or self-organised learning (for example, Siemens, 2005; Mitra et al, 2016). There are bodies of knowledge to be taught and learnt, and focused instruction is the best way to equip a child for life; digital networks are a distraction.

Having looked at more ideological stances on technology we finally turn to pragmatic criticisms and ask 'Where is the evidence of impact?'. The most well-known analysis of educational innovation is Hattie's (2013) meta-analysis of over 200 educational interventions resulting in a list of innovations most and least likely to be effective. Technology comes about midway in that list, its impact on outcomes barely above average. If education needs reform there are other innovations such as self-reporting of grades, classroom discussion and scaffolding which are likely to have more impact. The OECD Programme for International Student Assessment (PISA) results show something similar. The aim of these tests, which are carried out with cohorts of secondary school students worldwide, is to provide a snapshot of how education systems are doing. One report (OECD, 2015) found that despite the pervasiveness of ICT, its impact on student performance was mixed at best. Overall, PISA results show no appreciable improvements in student achievement in reading, mathematics or science in the countries that had invested heavily in ICT for education, this held true even when those tests in reading were configured to take better account of online contexts. The authors gave examples of systems with low access to computers but high reading outcomes and of ones with high access to computers with low reading outcomes to illustrate the point.

The OECD, which sponsors PISA, is, as we saw earlier, not dismissive of computers in education and argues for their use to keep up with economic and social change. Indeed, it also points out that online tools can help teachers and school leaders exchange ideas and inspire each other. However, in what appears an understatement it suggests that 'connections among students, computers and learning are neither simple nor hard-wired; and the real contributions ICT can make to teaching and learning have yet to be fully realised and exploited' (OECD, 2015: 15). A similar picture emerges in past systematic review into the impact of ICT. For example, answering the question 'What does forty years of research says about the impact of technology on learning?' Tamim et al (2011) found that the average effect size in their research ranged between 0.30 and 0.35, in other words 'low to moderate'. A systematic review with a more flexible methodology reached a similar conclusion (Higgins et al, 2012) and felt that 'it was difficult to identify clear and specific implications for educational practice in schools'. These findings have been substantiated in later reports.

Repeatedly researchers have found the impact of technology to be restricted. Of course this might be a consequence of the way that computers are used, and perhaps technology could have a much greater impact if it was used 'properly'. But after all these years where is the evidence that institutions can use technology 'properly'?. Is it simply asking too much for schools and other institutions to invest in the training and necessary support to make digital resources effective, safe and maintained? Schools are rarely resourced at comparable levels to commercial organisations and leaders have so many other issues demanding their attention than managing computer networks. Schools may be missing out by side-lining technology but for sceptics this is understandable as they have more manageable and more effective ways of improving learning outcomes.

Comparing optimistic and pessimistic perspectives

Having presented both sides of the picture I now look at the strengths and weaknesses of each case and suggest a way of presenting a more balanced view.

Optimistic and pessimistic stances of technology are underpinned by widely varying ideas about technology in general but also about the nature of knowledge, teaching and teachers, young people and consequences of technology use (see Table 6.1). Optimists see technology as essentially liberating, they are upbeat about the self-organisation of learning and see knowledge as unbounded; they also see a close association between education and the information society it serves. In contrast, pessimists see knowledge as bounded, experiences of technology as suspect; they extoll the role of the teacher as both subject knowledge and pedagogical expert and are sceptical about the impact of technology on learning outcomes. We consider these propositions in turn.

First, who is right on the issue of *technology*? Of course much depends on personal circumstance: it is easy to be optimistic about technology if you are going to have a live-saving operation only made possible by advances in medical science, easy to be pessimistic if you think too hard about the likelihood of a nuclear war at some time in the future. And it depends on who you are looking at. Both pessimists and optimists are at times looking at outliers. Pessimism seems to come from within the discipline of psychology, with its long-standing interest in neuroses and anxiety, while optimism seems more associated with education research with its focus on agency and

Table 6.1: Two contrasting views of technology and of its place in education

Domain	An optimistic view	A pessimistic view
Technology	Liberating, can be put to creative use, ever-developing	Addictive, displacing other kinds of activity, threatening to physical and psychological health
Knowledge	Unbounded: knowing how to access knowledge is more important than knowing as a personal possession	Bounded: general principles need to be learnt
Teaching	Learner-centred, problem-solving or challenge-based learning	Teacher-centred or at least teacher-mediated pedagogy
Teachers	Organisers of learner experiences	Subject matter experts
Schools and other institutions	Curriculum in urgent need of reform, stakeholders are holding back necessary change	Wary of change, the curriculum should not be shaped by a solely economic or political rationale
Young people	Digital immigrants, adept at using technology, can self-organise learning	Extensive digital experiences do not constitute learning
Impact of digital tools	Catalytic potential, impact cannot be evaluated using traditional criteria	Negligible in terms of helping to meet the core curriculum

child-centredness. Both are in danger of missing mainstream use. Moreover, pessimists in particular run the risk of associating many of the social ills they are reporting with technology itself, rather than our passive acceptance of it. A worrying consequence of this position is that it helps drive a self-fulfilling prophecy and may lead parents to believe that there is nothing that can be done about regulating their children's use of technology and teachers believing that they cannot manage children's learning on machines. But we are not powerless and we need a discourse that recognises we can make rational choices.

Second, *knowledge*. A weakness in the optimistic stance is the belief that collaboration around the screen creates new knowledge. As a learner you certainly can learn a lot from working in self-organised groups, be it F2F or at a distance; you might feel safe and feel supported by others, but does collaboration result in new knowledge as such? Just because participants are able to agree on ways of looking at problems does not mean they have followed rigorous processes or considered all alternative possibilities, in short, it does not mean that they are right.

Turning next to *teaching and teachers*, there is something suspect in the idea that knowledge is necessarily best learnt in chaotic, informal contexts. It is one thing to say that academics have underestimated the importance of informal learning, this is true, but quite another thing to say that what is learnt in a planned, formal way cannot have practical application. A key case here is literacy. Children can be taught to read and write in quite removed contexts but once literacy is acquired there are no limits to the uses to which it can be put. This means that a child who has learnt to read from printed text, even a dull reading scheme text, may be quite capable of reading from a screen and a child who has learnt to write on paper can make up sentences using a word processor. On the other hand, those resisting the use of technology in formal teaching are almost certainly missing something. There seems little wrong about teaching general principles in contexts to which children can relate. There is an inertia in many school systems which frustrates all attempts at reform. In desperation, techno-romantics argue that we can work around them. This is wrong. Of course, teachers like any profession are a mixed bag and schools and other institutions vary widely. However, the lesson from the experience of the COVID-19-related lockdown, to take a recent example, is that most learners benefit from teacher mediation and that, for many, learning was not 'self-organised'. Moreover, those without access to social and cultural capital suffered most of all.

There is power, then, in collaborative or peer learning but this needs to be coupled with a clear account of pedagogy. Garrison et al (2001) provided a useful term, 'teaching presence', rather than 'teacher presence', to indicate that some of the things that teachers do (triggering debate, introducing new resources, monitoring participation, attending to group processes, providing feedback, judging the suitability of resources, explaining key words, offering emotional encouragement, chasing absences, reflecting on outcomes, adapting curricula and so on) can be carried out by members of a group. This is fine, but it would be perverse to imagine from this (and Garrison et al do not) that teachers, themselves, have no role in problem-based learning or that their skills and expertise should be dismissed or repackaged as 'standing behind the children, admiring their work, acting fascinated and praising them as much as possible'. If pedagogical change is needed then reforming schools and developing the teaching workforce seems to be the only way forward, with all the difficulties and frustrations this involves. Side-lining teachers and institutions cannot be the solution.

What, next, about the *young people* that *schools* serve? Optimists make a poor case for reform when they take for granted that schools and other institutions need to resemble the societies, and the 'information society', in which they are based. For this argument to work proponents have had to present as benign a view as possible of technology in society, and they do this by generalising from trends which only apply to certain sectors of the economy. We need a more critical understanding of economic and technological change, noting the problems as well as opportunities. The optimistic case that young people do creative things when technology is there should not be assumed either (see the discussion in Case 6.2; Livingstone and Sefton-Green, 2016). The idea of digital immigrants seems superficially attractive but is, as many have pointed out, deeply mistaken as a concept as it presents a rose-tinted view of how young people use technology and contains a strong dose, not only of technological determinism, but also a kind of biological determinism.

Schools and other institutions are in important ways different to society. At their best they have a commitment to their members, a concern for participation of all and an optimism about students' agency which may be missing in other spheres of students' lives. None of this is to detract from the need for educational reform. There is a good case for changing the way that literacy is taught and the kinds of texts which learners should access and there is, for that matter, a very strong case for a focus on technology itself (for example, covering courses on programming, understanding of the social consequences of technology, the idea of globalisation, how to stay safe online and so on). There are good reasons to bring problem solving and challenge-based learning into the curriculum and for having schools help students reflect critically on what is means to live in a society with a global reach. The curriculum could be repacked along the four C's of critical thinking, creativity, communication and collaboration, rather than traditional subject teaching. However, within any reform the idea of a general education should not be lost.

Finally, the *impact of technology* on education. A more balanced way of assessing technology is needed. Outcomes are generally more mixed than often appears. For example, Cuban saw educational television as an expensive failure in the United States, but this was not always the view at the time. Schramm (1962), in one evaluation, suggested that children who had experienced educational television were achieving as well as children who had not. Another finding was that television was popular in the lower school but use and interest tailed off considerably in older age groups. There were also signs of a pedagogical development of teaching with educational television based around an understanding of its use as a sole method, partial method or teaching supplement. Overall teachers were favourably disposed towards television and more favourable when they had experience of it, less when not. Educational television did make a difference but ended up being an add-on for some teachers, not a game-changer. Schramm argued that 'under some conditions and used in some ways, it (educational television) can be highly effective' (1962: 165). This conclusion could be adapted to cover more or less any technology innovation, and for that matter any non-technology-based one that has followed since then. This seems simply realistic: why should technology compensate for all the other structural conditions that influence educational outcomes? Why should 'live classes' offer a step change in learning in remote regions in China? Under the right conditions they can help support left behind students but technology cannot in itself address structural problems of disadvantage – in rural China these include the phenomenon of parents migrating to the city for work, low economic resources and teachers leaving to go to more successful schools. Recognising the scale of the challenge is no reason to give up on technology use. However, it is a reason for offering a more focused strategy concentrating perhaps on applications which really look like they can make a difference and which do not impose unrealistic demands on teachers.

Case 6.2: Living and learning in the digital age (Livingstone and Sefton-Green, 2016)

What is this about?

The authors followed a class of 13-year-olds in an ethnically mixed London school over some months and sought to show aspects of children's lives both inside and outside school and the role of technologies in their lives in general. They noted that technology was a controversial social issue with suggestions that computer use was promoting anxiety and threatening mental and physical health. They felt that while concerns about technology needed to be taken seriously it was easy to get lost in the rhetoric and fail to see opportunities which technology offered young people.

How did they frame their observations?

They were interested in putting children's experiences in a wider context and noted that the stable institutions and traditional communities which once provided for welfare were 'in retreat'; work offered few lifetime guarantees and safety nets had been much reduced. A lot of responsibility was being handed down to individuals, social solidarity was weakened. They noted that individuals enjoyed some new freedoms, but choice itself 'has become burdensome', as the cost of mistakes fell on individuals.

If personal lives were full of tension so was the work of schools and teachers within these schools. In fact, there was a long-standing tension as the goal of the school was to attend to the life chances of all, when in practice life chances were reduced for some and raised for others. Further, schools were caught between their 'disciplinary goals', that is, they were expected to encourage social order but also expected to foster initiative, flexible thinking and assertiveness.

So what did they find?

They found that young teenagers often seemed to be absorbed in 'life with their friends, in their bedrooms, online, or inside the world created by their headphones'. It appeared that the more *offline* spaces were controlled, the more young people turned to online spaces and networks. They saw these spaces as arenas to 'conduct their identity work and to experiment with relationships, thereby also altering (or "remediating") how their relationships are enacted offline'.

The authors suggested that although young people were always online this made less difference than many might think. Young people could use the internet to get to know almost anyone, anywhere, but on the whole they 'stick to their own kind'. They could explore forms of knowledge from anywhere, but they 'stick to the top-ten Google hits, and their favourite sites include Amazon and eBay'. Technology gave them the opportunity to produce their own content, to create vlogs and write fan fictions but they largely 'consumed stuff made by others'. This had to be understood as shaped by their concerns about carrying the burden of risk and partly a lack of awareness of alternative ways of using social media.

What is valuable here?

What is important in this account is the sense of balance; yes, technology is changing lives but not as much as often reported. Technology is seen as double-edged: it offers a space for identity work, which is valuable, but this is not so much a reflection of the power of technology affordances as a consequence of the closing down of physical spaces. Most books about technology seem to concentrate on 'screen life'. In contrast, the authors here have a lot to say about the way young people live in general and the book is the better for it. There are real difficulties for young people living in these parts of London, and of course many other cities worldwide, and technology cannot make up for this.

What difficulties does it pose?

The book has a focus on both the macro, for example the discourses around young people, and the changes in economic outputs, and the micro, the observations of the class and interviews with study participants. This is a strength, but it is difficult at times to see the way the macro and the micro levels are joined up or assess the evidence that one is connected to the other.

Summary

This chapter has covered different narratives around technology and I have:

- shown that there has been a great deal of optimism expressed about the use of technology in society;
- suggested that optimists offer a technologically determinist view of change and romanticise the impact of technology;

- shown that the pessimistic case is varied; some writers see technology as undermining the traditional role of teachers and institutions, some see drawbacks of excessive screen time and others point to a lack of demonstrable impact; and
- put forward a balanced view which accepts the need for education reform while offering a more critical and focused strategy for using technology to support change.

Where to read more

Informal learning is important and was much neglected by educationalists. Lave's (1977) original case study of traditional apprenticeship training in West Africa was influential in redressing this imbalance. Her point was that informal learning had been underestimated, she did not show that general or formal teaching was inherently ineffective.

One of the most optimistic and influential voices on the use of technology was that of Papert (for example, Papert, 1980, 1993). I have not discussed his ideas as they have been covered in depth in many places, but go to the 'Children's Machine' (Papert, 1993) for a characteristically upbeat account of technology in education, peppered with pessimism when he realises that schools are not going to change. If interested in debates over the language laboratory and language learning, the Keating (1963) report is an important early critique. The report was itself heavily criticised (for example, Conwell, 1964).

I offer a summary of different stances on education (these cover progressive, conservative, neoliberal, reformist and radical positions) in Hammond and Wellington (2019). Reese (2001) gives a historical view of progressivism while Hirsch (2010) is the key text for conservatives.

Buckingham in several publications has offered a balanced view of media and its application in the curriculum (for example, Buckingham, 2007a, 2007b).

Much of popular thinking about technology has been framed by its representation in books and films. For example, science fiction has offered both optimistic (utopian) and pessimistic (dystopian) visions of the technological future at various times (see Klein et al, 1977, and a short but informative overview by Steinmueller, 2017). My interest in the film *2001: A Space Odyssey* was triggered by Latour (2002) who referenced it to support his view that tools are almost animate, as he puts it, '[t]hose who believe that tools are simple utensils have never held a hammer in their hand, have never allowed themselves to recognize the flux of possibilities that they are suddenly able to envisage' (2002: 250). Latour recognises the destructive power of technology; we can never 'master it'. Much of the pessimism around today's use of technology is focused on surveillance capitalism (see Lyon, 2019, as an introduction).

Academics have been quick to report on the lockdown associated with the COVID-19 pandemic, see, for example, Leask and Younie (2021). There is a lot written about PISA, for example, Sellar et al (2017). The website for PISA is found at http://www.oecd.org/pisa/

7

How can we theorise better?

In this book I set out to inquire into the state of theorising about technology in education and in this final chapter I reflect back on what has been covered and suggest ways in which we can improve the way we theorise. The chapter is divided into three sections:

- What then is theory?
- Developing a research community
- How can we theorise better?

What then is theory?

In the book I have explored both theory and theorising, before going on to look at the ways in which research has been carried out in learning with technology, teaching with technology and technology itself. Many of the examples presented in the book concern technology in schools but informal learning, general engagement with technology, professional learning, pre-school and post-school settings are also there. There are areas I could have gone into in greater depth (for example, using AI; technology in particular subject areas; virtual presence and embodiment; policy making; the 'Internet of Things') but there is only so much room. As it is, the range of examples enables me to say some things about theory and emphasise again the different meanings attached to it. Indeed, in Chapter 1 I suggested that theory should not be associated with a single kind of research activity; whenever we are noticing and explaining patterns in the use of technology backed up using concepts and ideas from a wider field of study then we are making theory. This very flexible and inclusive view means that many different types of output can be seen as theoretical (see Table 7.1).

Theory works by saying what the important elements are in an intervention or phenomenon and how these different elements fit together. All the examples of research in Table 7.1 achieved this. For example, Teague et al (2015) picked out three stages of development in programming; Ertmer (2005) identified factors that influenced take-up of ICT; Cole and Engeström (1993) offered a model of an activity system; and Nikolaidou (2012) modelled collaborative interactions. Four different kinds of contributions over time but each allowing what was learnt in one study to be transferred to another.

Table 7.1: Examples to illustrate various types of theoretical contribution

Type of contribution	Examples of theoretical outputs
A conceptualisation of a phenomenon	*Chapter 1* TPCK (Mishra and Koehler, 2006) Familiar routines (Olson, 1988) *Chapter 3* Computer meets school, school wins (Cuban, 2001) First- and second-order factors (Ertmer, 2005) *Chapter 4* Social shaping of technology (MacKenzie and Wajcman, 1999) Internet of Things (Kassab et al, 2020) *Chapter 5* Hybridity (Eyal and Gil, 2022; Lindtner et al, 2008) *Chapter 6* Surveillance capitalism (Zuboff, 2019) Digital nativism (Prensky, 2001) The second screen (Turkle, 2005)
Typologies	*Chapter 1* Three (plus one) 'paradigms' of software design (MacDonald, 1977) Categories of online interaction (Agudo-Peregrina et al, 2014) *Chapter 4* Responses to innovation (Rogers, 2010) Types of school leadership (Bush and Glover, 2014) *Chapter 5* Affordances of Web 2.0 (Conole and Dyke, 2004)
Conceptual frameworks or models	*Chapter 1* TAM (Davis) Unplugging (Morris and Cravens Pickens, 2017) *Chapter 3* Three stages of development in programming (Teague et al, 2015) Collaborative interactions model (Nikolaidou, 2012) 'Distributed' view learning (Perkins, 1993) Networked learning (Jones, 2015) Affinity spaces (Gee, 2018) CoI (Garrison et al, 2001) *Chapter 4* Arena framework (Davis et al, 2019) *Chapter 5* ANT/CoP framework (Johannesen and Habib, 2010)
Testing hypotheses	*Chapter 1* Do online forums make a difference? (Kang and Zhang, 2020) Do students using HMD based interactive video learn more? (Hamilton et al, 2021). *Chapter 3* Does TAM predict ICT take-up? (Teo and Milutinovic, 2015). Can we predict at-risk students using learning analytics? (Hung et al, 2019)

Table 7.1: Examples to illustrate various types of theoretical contribution (continued)

Type of contribution	Examples of theoretical outputs
	Does instruction software improve learning outcomes? (Banerjee et al, 2007)
	Chapter 4 Can we say what exemplary teachers who use ICT look like? (Becker, 1994)
Action-oriented experiments with technology	*Chapter 1* Do technology-assisted urban games have potential? (Pitura and Terlecka-Pacut, 2018) How can we support students' information literacy? (Supriyadi et al, 2020)
	Chapter 3 What happens when parents and children jointly play computer games? (Siyahhan et al, 2010)
	Chapter 4 Can language students co-operate across borders? (Blin and Appel, 2011)
	Chapter 5 How can we use IT for democratic purposes? (Bentley et al, 2019)
	Chapter 6 Can children learn from interaction with Robot Julia? (Yueh and Chiang, 2020) What happens if you provide a computer in the wall? (Mitra et al, 2016) Can we create purposeful online communities? (Rheingold, 1993)
What ought/ought not to be?	*Chapter 1* Schools need to keep up (Mogas et al, 2022) We need to be aware of a surveillance culture (Kwet, 2017) We need to be connected (Siemens, 2005) We need to by-pass formal education if possible (Mitra et al, 2016)
	Chapter 6 Teachers need to change (Prensky, 2001) Less screen time (Greenfield, 2015)
An analysis of key thinkers and ideas	*Chapter 1* Transactional knowledge (Hickman, 2009) Feminist methodology (Clegg and Trayhurn, 2000)
	Chapter 3 Behaviourism/cognitive theory/social constructivism (Vygotsky and Cole, 1978) CoP (Lave and Wenger, 1991) CHAT (Cole and Engeström, 1993)
	Chapter 4 Ecological theory (Bronfenbrenner, 1979) Zones framework (Valsiner, 1997)
	Chapter 5 Affordances (Gibson, 1986)
	Chapter 6 Critical Theory (Feenberg, 2017)

In Chapter 1, I raised the criticisms made about technology in education research: it was flat, swayed by novelty, going through the motions, overblown, technologically determinist and over-optimistic. I asked 'Are these criticisms fair?'. Well, it all depends on where you look. It is not difficult to find examples which provide fuel for the critics. On the plus side, however, there really are strengths to the research of technology in education and I have included examples of vibrant, cross-disciplinary and critical work. A further strength of the field, and of education research in general, is the close association between researchers and practitioners. This means that a teacher could find in the academic literature ideas on promoting information literacy, making provision for remote or hard-to-reach learners, encouraging productive talk around technology, supporting students' programming skills and so on which would help inform their practice. However, not all of the studies I have included in the book represent good examples of theorising and three difficulties in particular stand out.

First, if theory abstracts from the data this means that we have to have relevant data in the first place. In most examples this was the case, though I did criticise, particularly in some learning analytics work, a tendency to go 'fishing' for data and see what turns up. We also saw that some rather optimistic statements about the way young people used technology were made by generalising from atypical cases. A lot was made about young people as digital immigrants (for example, Prensky, 2001), about the creativity participants exhibit in online affinity spaces (Gee, 2018), or learners' capacity to self-organise (for example, Siemens, 2005; Mitra et al, 2016) which I argued underplayed variations in participation patterns, the asymmetry in power and prestige among learners and groups of learners and the quality of interaction. From an opposite perspective, I also found that too much was made of anxiety and health risks caused by screen time by focusing on those who were 'addicted' (for example, Greenfield, 2015). Atypical cases form part of the picture, but it would be wrong to assume that, first, all young people have the same relationship to technology and, second, that all have access to the same tools and resources. To be fair, sometimes readers are themselves doing the over-generalising and miss that researchers explain they are dealing with emerging rather than general patterns of behaviour. For example, Turkle was one of the first to draw attention to the value of screen time for young people but as she herself pointed out this conclusion was based on an atypical sample: 'The people I describe in the chapters on computer cultures are not "average" computer users. Computers are a larger part of their lives than for most people. I write about them in order to present portraits of what can happen when people enter very close relationships with this machine' (Turkle, 2005: 25).

Second, the story of technology use can be 'over-determined', so that, say, models such as unplugging (Morris et al, 2017) or, on a much more general scale, CHAT (Cole and Engeström, 1993), which are there to help readers think through a process, become seen as the process set in stone. This is perhaps inevitable as theories are drawing attention to what is key in a study; they cannot cover everything and inevitably the picture they present is a simplification. However, nuance is possible and it was helpful when writers were clear that users may see technology in different ways (Johannesen and Habib, 2010, is a really good example of this) and that technology necessarily comes with a mix of opportunity and constraint (see the discussion of affordances in Chapter 4). Feenberg (2017) suggested (see Chapter 6) that we should avoid presenting the development of technology as a story of what was inevitable, but there have been very few explicit examples of researchers offering alternative perspectives on their findings. Cuban et al (2001) were, however, refreshingly open that the data could be seen in a different way but this did not stop them from offering a very stark picture of the lack of impact of ICT. In contrast, Olson (1988), a very good study in many respects and one which shows the value of going back to past literature, celebrated the role of routines in teachers' work. As we saw in Chapter 1 this really challenged the view, often repeated since, that technology is positively disruptive, in other words that disruption is an unequivocally 'good thing'. But there was a different way of looking at Olson's example: Could routines sometimes hold back teachers from trying new things out or reflecting on what they had? Could it lead to complacency?

Third, there were gaps when it came to supporting explanations. In Chapter 2 'narrow' was contrasted with 'wide' explanation: narrow explanation stuck closely to the data when providing models or conceptualisations, but wide explanation brought in a range of literature as backing. The weakness of narrow explanation was that it was too tightly bounded and so did not contribute to a wider narrative around technology. One example of this, as discussed in Chapter 4, was the 'factors approach' to teacher take-up of ICT – factors A, B and C were observed in one study, B, C and D in another, C, D and E in a third. This tradition has some obvious benefits but does not give a dynamic picture of teacher decision-making or say very much about the changing context in which teachers work.

A more general problem, particularly in many deductive studies, is the priority given to noting associations between variables and the relative neglect of explanation. Researchers of technology acceptance will describe degrees of association between, say, ease of use and intention to use technology to three decimal places but then offer only the most cursory comments as to why any association should exist. This was also a problem in some learning analytics research which showed, say, a relationship between gender and participation in an online course but had little to say about gender and society in the first place. Of course, such neglect of wider theory is not a necessary condition of learning analytics research and a study by Jovanovic et al (2021) was singled out for showing how learning theory could inform the planning of a research project as well as provide backing for an explanation at the end of that project.

Developing a research community

If there are strengths and weakness in past studies what can we say about the research field as a whole? The first thing to state here is that while I have referred throughout to a 'technology in education' research community, I am not sure that a coherent research community exists. Thus, in this last section I offer some ideas as to what such a community might look like. In particular, I want to see a research community that is more theoretically informed, while remaining inclusive. In this community members will look at, and be enthused by, what is new but also be interested in the history of technology. They will keep a distinctively critical and educational focus throughout. These ideas are discussed in turn.

The community will be more theoretically informed

To become more theoretically informed, the research community will need to show a deeper engagement with the literature, but where exactly to look? In fact, researchers seem to be getting their ideas from four main fields (see Table 7.2):

- *Educational technology*. Researchers go here to access generally optimistic views about technology use and a picture of technology as new and positively disruptive. In this field fall ideas such as distributed learning, connectivism, TPCK and self-organising systems, all of which appear as go-to resources for new researchers.
- *Education*. Here researchers see traditional concerns for curriculum, subject pedagogy, policy and leadership as important and applicable to the research of technology. Researchers often draw on cognitive and constructivist learning theory to explain what is happening in the classroom (for example, Bulfin et al, 2013) and see the idea of educational reform as important for promoting the take-up of ICT.
- *Cognate*. These are fields which have a subsidiary focus on education within a wider concern for social organisations in general or for computers and computing. They include fields of computer science, media studies and anthropology, as well as sub-fields such as child development, innovation and culture, management studies, organisational studies and professional learning, among many others. Delving into these areas enable ideas of informal learning and apprenticeship, community of practice, ecological systems, activity theory and so on to be brought into the discussion of technology use.

Table 7.2: Examples of the provenance of concepts and theories used in technology in education research

Field	Examples of concepts
Educational technology	Affinity groups Connectionism Digital nativism Factors in take-up of ICT Information literacy Knowledge building Learning analytics Networked learning Self-organising system TPCK
Education	Cognitivism Cooperation and collaboration Play School leadership and school reform Social constructionism Subject pedagogy
Cognate	Big Data (data science) CHAT (innovation studies) Community of practice (anthropology, organisation studies) Ecological theory (child development) Human Computer Interaction (anthropology, computing, psychology) Internet of Things (computer science) Social shaping of technology (sociology) TAM (organisational studies)
Social science disciplines	Affordance (psychology) ANT (sociology) Capital (sociology) Contact hypothesis (social psychology) Modernity, postmodernity (politics/sociology) Surveillance (politics) and surveillance capitalism (economics)

- *Social science disciplines*. These are fields which allow more general ideas to be brought into the study of technology, for example surveillance, disinformation and citizenship (politics), theories of capital and of science and technology (sociology), affordances, anxiety, addiction, theories of reasoned action (psychology), digital capitalism (economics) and so on.

Do any of these fields offer new researchers in education more insight than others? I do not think so, it depends entirely on the research interests and the research questions that are being asked. For example, questions about perception suggest an excursion into social psychology, questions about technology's contribution of learning lead into learning theory, questions about context may bring in the cognate field of organisational theory, questions about computers and programming will fit best with computer studies. However, there is one overriding conclusion when it comes to drawing on resources: studies appear more convincingly theorised when researchers are prepared to spread their gaze wider than the narrowly defined field of educational technology. Educational technology research can appear over-optimistic and carries a general air of technocentrism when it comes to discussing young people. Researchers who take a wider perspective offer important insight. For example, the study cited earlier on mobile phone use in Sri Lanka (Wijetunga, 2014) is given depth by drawing on Bourdieu; Johannesen and Habib's (2010) study of VLEs is strengthened by reference to ANT; and Livingstone and Sefton-Green's (2016) book is transformed from a descriptive account of how students use technology to a theoretical one by their more general discussion of the literature on the consequences of neoliberalism. These and other studies work as researchers have adapted general frameworks to fit their context; in other words the point is to draw on theories, not to use theories unthinkingly. Indeed, in the case of Wijetunga and Johannesen and Habib different frameworks have been merged creatively: in Wijetunga concepts of affordance and Bourdieu's concept of capital; in Johannesen and Habib concepts of CoP and ANT.

It will value different kinds of contributions

I return to a point made in Chapter 1 that theory is not the be-all and end-all of academic endeavour; we should avoid lambasting researchers for weak theorisation when theorisation might not have been their goal. In a changing field such as technology research there is a real need for description as we need to know what is happening before we can get on with theorising about why it is happening. Descriptive surveys such as the one cited of young people in Europe (see Smahel, 2020) provide an important service, as does the 'whole class' sampling in Livingstone and Sefton-Green (Case 6.2). Indeed, Livingstone and Sefton-Green's picture of young people using technology for identity work while 'sticking to their own kind' and largely 'consuming stuff made by others' is extremely helpful for puncturing both optimistic and pessimistic accounts of technology.

If we are to develop into an inclusive community, work within different methodological traditions will be valued and assessed on its own terms. I have made criticism of deductive studies for being circular and for using theories 'off-the-peg'. However, this need not be the case. Venkatesh et al (2003) present a counter-example when seeking a unified theory of acceptance and use of technology (UTUAT). Here researchers reviewed eight different models of technology acceptance and identified 32 constructs across the eight models. They also found key moderating variables. However, they also noted some limitations of the studies they had reviewed, for example, the studies focused on more basic applications, they were post-hoc studies, they were biased to commercial contexts, they looked too much at intention to use software and not actual use. They were then able to trial and review models with expert panels before testing their own unified model in four different contexts involving the actual use of technology. This was all critical and highly theoretical work, very different from researchers who simply take a likely looking theory, such as UTUAT, on trust.

Meanwhile, inductive studies, and the in-depth case studies that are typical of this methodological approach, can be difficult to relate to beyond their particular context. Case studies, must do more than describe and many do. For example, *hybridity*, *unplugging*, perhaps ideas of *assimilation* and *accommodation* are concepts that came from close observation of events, or descriptions of events, but take on a wider significance and have greater explanatory power. Case studies can be theoretical as well as having practical application. A good example here is a study of music composition discussed earlier (Nikolaidou, 2012). This showed the value of music composition software for enabling 'provisionality and iteration', in other words the technology allowed students to easily play back and re-work their tunes. However, provisionality and iteration are not invariant features of the software but they can be observed when the software is used in an appropriate way. These observations enable a pedagogical focused discussion of technology but without the technocentric overtones.

It will use the past to understand the present

In Chapter 1, I suggested that a theoretical contribution offers something new. However, being new does not rule out exploring the past and theorising is only made possible by drawing on resources which have been handed down to us, even if these resources needed to be understood and creatively adapted.

An interesting example here is that of TPCK. Mishra and Koehler (2006) drew on earlier work by Shulman (1986), but those using TPCK rarely go back that far. In fact Shulman was interested in the varying conceptions policy makers had about learning to teach. He noted that over time there has been a shift of focus from mastery of the subject (content knowledge) towards (and he was writing in the United States) pedagogical knowledge. A problem was that we were seeing knowledge in either/or terms: either we had teachers who knew how to teach or teachers who knew their subject content. As Shulman saw it, we should be having both subject knowledge plus teacher know-how. Furthermore, an understanding of curriculum knowledge, for example, knowledge of what is being assessed and how to support particular learning outcomes, was also needed. Shulman alerts us to subtleties in describing teacher knowledge as well; it consists not just of formal propositional knowledge but makes use of metaphors to frame teaching practice.

From Shulman then we see the importance of 'reflexivity' – an awareness that we are always making subjective judgements when we describe teacher knowledge and that teacher knowledge is subject to fashion. We also learn that it is very difficult to codify, still less operationalise, content and pedagogic knowledge. In fact, Shulman sees possibilities for evaluating teacher knowledge by establishing long-term researcher–teacher relationships, making extended conversations and observation of the classroom possible. These are really helpful insights, yet there many studies into teachers' use of technology which ignore Shulman altogether. In some of these studies instruments are used to 'measure' TPCK in self-reported surveys and teacher knowledge is treated as though it can be captured without the researcher ever going into a classroom, which was not what Shulman had in mind at all. The result is that these papers on TPCK are unconvincing: researchers seem to have an instrument for measuring TPCK, they use this instrument for measuring TPCK before and after an intervention, and 'hey presto' the data shows that teachers know more TPCK at the end than at the start of the intervention. This kind of approach is circular and has little to add to theorisation of teacher knowledge.

One troubling aspect of technology research is the idea that learning with digital tools becomes qualitatively different to anything that has gone before. Everything is new: the tools are new; learning is new; contexts are new (see Prensky, 2001; Siemens, 2005). Yet such a stance does not ring true when we consider how, as social beings, we have lived and learnt over time. Ever since we lived in caves we have shown each other how to use tools, practised the use of these tools, talked aloud about how we can adapt tools to new contexts.

The world has changed, media change, the way we write about learning changes, but the fundamental process of sharing knowledge is surely not that different. To take an example mentioned in Chapter 5: the game of chess has been influenced by AI, particularly at an elite level where each new variation is run past a computer program. For the social player, the game has been extended and enhanced through discussion within social networks, playing against computer programs, accessing tutorials and guidance on video-sharing sites, and most of all the opportunity to find someone anywhere around the world to play against via the internet. However, learning the game is the same as it ever was. The beginner needs someone to explain the rules, needs to practise, to get feedback from a more knowledgeable other, reflect on weaknesses and strengths, practise some more and go on to participate in a chess-playing community. Such a beginner would, we imagine, make use of internet tools and technology, that part is new, but they will serve an apprenticeship in the same way as anyone who has played the game has done in the past. Of course, contexts and media are different, but technology research appears more convincing when it can trace back to past educational principles rather than start with a blank page. Garrison et al (2001) in their discussion of community of inquiry and Teague et al (2015) in looking at computer programming are good examples of taking a longer view.

It will be critical

Members will offer more nuanced views of technology, making it clear that learners and teachers will use digital tools in different ways, including ways not envisaged by their designers or by those who promote their use. Learners and teachers may eschew the use of a tool altogether. *Where* technology is used will be investigated as much as *how* it is used.

Members will make well-informed critical comments about the inertia of educational systems but also question the technological determinism that sees computers as the answer to problems of access, engagement and accreditation. Some of the time members will work productively with those promoting technology in education. However, at other times researchers may need to stand on the side and remind policy makers of what did not work in the past and what is unlikely to work now. They must be prepared to say it is more complicated than you think.

Members will be sceptical of accounts which see users as having unbounded agency. Attempts to allow for both agency and structure are, of course, methodologically complex but there are resources to draw on. For example, ecological framing in its broadest sense looked helpful (see Chapter 4) and ANT, for all its shortcomings, has really helped the theorising of technology by showing that tools have evolved under the influence of the social groups that use them. Technology is, or at least can be thought of, as a player, or actor, in a social system. As for social framing, Bourdieu's idea that there are different kinds of capital which shape social activity seems helpful and this is enhanced by the accompanying concepts of habitus (how our life experiences develop within us habits, skills and dispositions) and field (implicit and explicit rules of behaviour, and valuations put on that behaviour in particular sites of activity). To be clear, the community will not be defined by an interest in one particular theory or theorist but will explore how questions of agency have been framed in other disciplines and how they can be re-worked for technology mediation. As an educational community, members will also have a distinctive concern for informed agency, and how they can help promote learners' freedom to act while understanding the consequences of their actions for others.

It will be an educational community

Members of the community will have a special interest in education and in the problems within both formal education (curriculum, leadership, pedagogy and so on) as well as informal learning in families, communities and the professions. Education research is interested in practical application in ways that discipline research is not. This does not make it atheoretical, or disinterested in sociological, economic or other discipline theory, but theory has to be there for a reason: to help address problems of practice. At times, this concern for practice will lead researchers to take part in their own action-oriented projects, including participatory or design thinking experiments alongside more traditional action research. At other times, indeed many other times, researchers will use conventional methodologies. However, they will always seek the involvement of practitioners and other stakeholders, and will spell out the implications of their research for their audiences.

Further, researchers will be concerned about the ethical issues which education poses. Enlightenment values tell us that people share a common humanity and have the same right to develop their life chances. There are obvious reasons why this does not happen, but educationalists need to take fairness seriously. The research community is there to remind everyone that over a third of the world's population do not have access to the internet and there are social and cultural conditions which constrain access in its wider sense and pervert its application in unhealthy ways. The research community cannot solve these issues but it can puncture unrealistic discourse. Members will want to help institutions develop sustainable developments in technology that make a difference.

Members will be interested in, and indeed enthused about, technology but recognise that their main focus is on education and this will lead them to ask different questions to computer scientists. For example, imagine a world in which neural machine translation devices are so advanced that people could be provided with a small digital device implanted, say, in their neck which enabled seamless, reliable and apparently authentic communication in more or less any language used across the world. With such an implant you could quite literally say that you possess language skills. Making this happen would be an interesting focus for computer science research. Indeed such an invention may be achievable – translation devices have been impressive to date albeit they have proved problematic when it comes to expressing subtlety. However, technology in education researchers have a rather different role. They are there to explore the consequences of such a device for education and for society as whole, but they are also there to say 'wait a minute this implant has enabled you to use to another language, but you have not learnt a language'. Learning requires active effort, it is not simply something that one possesses but something that has been worked at. This is not to downplay the importance of technology advances, but it is to stress that educationalists must be able to say what learning is and what it is not.

How can we theorise better?

Description has its place but if we really want to push ourselves into theorising about technology in education how should we do it? I finish on some more pragmatic suggestions for the planning, analysis and presenting of research.

Planning for theorising

Ask searching research questions

Researchers ask a great many precise questions that yield largely descriptive answers: What do teachers think about this tool? What do students think? How do teachers use X in the classroom? Do students who access X do better than students who access Y? These are all good questions which guide the researcher when choosing between surveys, interviews, experimental testing and so on as methods. But when it comes to theorising more abstract open-ended questions are needed *as well*. For example: What is the nature of teacher knowledge about technology? What is distinctive in contemporary childhood? How do we feel presence when online? Why should TAM be considered a useful model for teacher take-up? If we only address the descriptive questions we will end up with a descriptive study, or at best a narrow kind of explanation.

Reflect deeply on your theoretical framework

Theoretical frameworks play a different role in deductive and inductive studies but whichever approach is taken it is important to critically review previous models and theories. Do not take theories on trust, each comes with flaws and they were not designed for your particular research context.

Don't feel bound by deductive and inductive categories

In a deductive approach the researcher makes use of previous studies and this makes it easier to see how the findings fit into the field. The flip-side is that there is a strong tendency towards replication and an over-commitment to one way of looking at the problem. In contrast, inductive approaches seem more creative and more likely to result in fresh theorisation. However, they run the risk of being excessively time-consuming, and ending up re-inventing what was already known. The problems in both traditions can be addressed by an iterative approach, testing out conceptions and adapting as the research proceeds.

Follow the theory back

When alighting on a concept or theory that looks like it might be relevant, trace it back. For example, suppose you found a reference to Dewey in a study of online problem-based learning, ask yourself how is Dewey being used in support of this approach? Do a bit of detective work. Look at other cases, not just technology studies, in which Dewey has been evoked: Is Dewey being interpreted in the same way across these studies? Go back to the original sources. You will not have time to read everything, and in Dewey's case this would be a lifetime undertaking, but at least go back to the original chapter in which a citation or quote appears. What picture do you get now and how, if at all, can this help in conceptualising your project? Remember, this is not about setting yourself up to be an expert on Dewey, rather you are seeking to become a balanced and informed commentator on how one of Dewey's ideas has (or has not) an application in technology related research.

Follow the approach back

There is always a precursor. If theorising about live classes, at least be aware of experiments in educational television (for example, Schramm, 1962; Cuban, 1986). If you are interested in MOOCs, look up what was said about correspondence courses and later about old-style open university distance learning; if you are interested in learning analytics look at how institutions have used (or not used) data in the past; if you think digital technology makes young people different then look at what older generations have said about young people. The trick is to work out what is new and what is constant.

Follow the technology back

Try to trace what the designers said about their software, and perhaps hardware. For example, where did the idea of an IWB come from? Why did policy makers promote their use in the classroom? What happened when they were introduced? How did use become routinised in a certain way? This will highlight how certain uses have become accepted within a system and others rejected.

Analysing and theorising
Explain your findings

Theorising sets out to explain why there was an association between X or Y, why X was a consequence of Y. If you found that teachers avoided using a particular programme or student outcomes were improved by following a particular approach, where can you look for support for this finding? Is there a theory of learning that backs you up? This might be a theory of collaboration, perhaps a theory of resilience, or it might be a theory of technology or a theory of organisational behaviour. You cannot cover all the bases so ask yourself what appears most powerful. Be careful not to simply throw in a reference to a theorist – remember to follow the theory itself back.

Identify both opportunity and constraint

Technology brings both opportunity and drawbacks, and I argue that you cannot have one without the other. Social media has widened reach but it has also shepherded us into echo chambers; IWBs lead to better presentations but also more didactic teaching; technology provides flexibility but this flexibility creates anxiety. Watch out for the relentlessly positive or negative theories of technology and try to strike a balance.

See it from other points of view

Keep an open mind that there are alternative explanations for your data. Try to see the same findings using a different model or conceptual frame. For example, what would your study of teacher take-up look like if viewed from an ecological rather than an activity theory perspective? Why should you go for one rather than the other?

Accept that theorising is in part guesswork

Research proceeds slowly step by step but theorising, or at least the picture of theorising offered by Swedberg (2012, 2016) and others, involves a leap of the imagination leading to a more abstract conceptualisation. Be brave. The concepts you introduce are plausible best fits which do not tell the truth of study but a way of looking at the study.

Give yourself time and space

There is serendipity; theories do not emerge out of thin air but you do need to step away from the study and think in a different way. You really need to 'unplug' – both metaphorically and digitally – to theorise, give yourself time to reflect.

Give thought to your positionality

We all have a position, which leads us to identify problems as worthy of research and we all see data and theories in different ways. Positionality is often talked about as a threat to research objectivity but without a position we could not make sense of the world in the first place; it is virtue as well as vice. But you do need to be aware of how your position affects the way you theorise and what you theorise about. If you are from the global north it is easy to make sweeping statements about the role of computers in modern life which ignores the experience of many people in the global south, and if you are an interested and capable technology user it is easy to miss the reservations that others have about technology.

Presenting theories

Use language carefully

Be as precise as you can when explaining the influence of technology. If you want to talk about 'technology addiction' then check that is what you mean, rather than there are people who use technology a lot, more so than they would like. Ask yourself whether technology *causes* something to happen, *leads to* something happening, *influences* something, and whether society *determines, shapes, frames, constrains* technology use. If you are dealing with factors explain whether these factors are *causal, contextual* or *mediating*.

When it comes to technical words, explain what you understand by them. Use popular terms such as digital immigrants, Gen Z, millennials carefully, or better not at all. They are broad, they can unhelpfully stereotype and they are generated within the global north but assumed to be globally relevant. Be critical of the shifting vocabulary around technology, this can confuse as much as help. Avoid disparaging language. Is 'laggard' the right word for describing people who do not want to use technology? Why should quiet learners be configured as 'lurkers' with its connotations of seediness?

Focus on what is important

Theories work best by abstracting out what is important in a situation, try not to overwhelm with the detail. Use diagrams if they help you and your readers understand the way the various elements in your study work together but be aware they may be subject to over-interpretation. They are representations of what happened and not the complete picture.

Summary

In this final chapter I have:

- reiterated the idea that theory is at heart it is about providing an explanation backed up using concepts and ideas from a wider field of study;
- shown that there are strengths in 'technology in education' research but also weaknesses, in particular when it comes to theorising. These

include over-generalising from atypical cases, seeing technology use as over-determined, leaving gaps when searching for backing of claims;
- argued for a more theoretically informed, critical, education-focused research community; and
- shown how theorising comes into each stage of the research process.

Key terms

Action research   seeks to address social and professional problems through repeated cycles of planning, taking action and reflection on action. Action research can be considered as a kind of a practitioner inquiry. Action research has been important in the field of education and other professional contexts, its popularity varying over time.

Activity   in the context of social research, activity is what people do to make something happen, and can be contrasted with behaviour, which is more associated with how actions are triggered by external conditions.

Activity theory   a commonly used framework for theorising social activity in which activity is seen as mediated by both physical and symbolic tools. A wider view of activity theory (CHAT) was developed, most notably by Engeström and colleagues to suggest that that activity takes place within a system of rules, community and division of labour.

Actor network theory (ANT)   a framework for explaining social activity as arising from networks of humans and non-human 'actors'. ANT often has a focus on how networks are created and maintained and how, once created, networks become taken for granted.

Agency   concerns the extent to which individuals can act independently and to make their own decisions unencumbered by material or cultural constraint. Agency can be seen as a licence for free expression but exercising agency involves awareness of our situation, the range of responses open to us and the likely consequences of our actions for others. The idea of responsible agency informs education literature.

Analysis   refers to the breaking down of a topic or object into its component parts and understanding how those parts fit together.

Artefacts	refers to objects, both tools and cultural products, made by human beings. It has associations with the historic past, for example, archaeologists report on the artefacts they dig up, however it is used in a more general sense in technology studies, for example, digital presentations are artefacts.
Artificial intelligence (AI)	AI systems seek to simulate human intelligence processes. AI systems identify patterns in large sets of data. For example, an image recognition tool can learn to identify and describe images by reviewing millions of examples. There are strong and weak applications of AI in education. Weaker applications require human input, for example, voice activation.
Audiences	individuals, practitioners, academics, public and private groups or organisations to whom research is addressed.
Behaviourism	a learning theory that stresses the importance of accurate practice and giving positive reinforcement of correct responses.
Big Data	can simply refer to very large data files, but is more often used to describe constantly updated data, for example Twitter feeds, blog posts, sensor readings. Data may be collected without a specific purpose in mind, for example logs of past viewing history, which then turn out to have useful applications for researchers. Big Data is defined by the three V's: velocity (the speed with which data are collected and updated); volume (the sheer extent of data); and variety (the different types of data).
Causality	posits a relationship between a cause (X) and an effect (Y) so that X can be said to result in Y. The direction of influence is important: X should precede Y. A causal explanation needs to show why X causes Y, there is more than just an association between X and Y. In practice most research deals in loose kinds of causality, 'on the balance of probability Y is likely to result from X'.

Challenge based learning   the idea of using real-world or at least simulated real-world problems to promote collaborative and hands-on learning, the approach lies in the tradition of problem-based learning.

Cognitivism   seeks to provide explanations as to how we receive, organise and retrieve information in our minds, that is, it seeks to understand internal mental processes. It often sees learners as active in the process of learning.

Collaboration   usually seen as a process leading to jointly constructed artefacts or achievements. *Cooperation* is a process leading to an assembled product, that is, each member of the team does their part of the task. However the terms are not used consistently.

Concepts   units of meaning formed by comparing, and abstracting, common characteristics from different cases.

Conceptual framework   sets out the key variables or issues in a study. In an inductive enquiry a conceptual *framing* may be loose and speculative but in deductive enquiry the *framework* may provide the basis for the hypothesis being tested.

Connectivism   a theory which sees learning as 'chaotic' and an outcome of reflection from participation in many different networks.

Constructivism   provides a focus on how individuals, or individuals in groups (*social* constructivism), make meaning; in contrast to behaviourism the world is seen as made up of constructions rather than objective realities.

Correlation   the degree of association or dependence between two variables so that X can be said to be associated with Y. Correlation is not synonymous with causality.

Counterfactual   what might have happened if events had been different. For example, imagine a totally reformed education system.

Critical Theory	a concern for understanding the shortcomings of a system and the potential for something much better, draws on ideas emanating from the Frankfurt school in Germany.
Criticality	involves the exercise of careful and well-informed judgement and offering one's stance after taking into account of numerous competing views.
Culture	achievements in the arts and humanities, but more usually in social research what is shared in terms of attitudes, values and practices among members of groups or institutions, expressed colloquially as 'the way things are done'.
Data	in Latin datum is 'what is given', hence the idea that data are what we have to work with. In information systems data are contrasted with information and knowledge: data are raw, information involves making meaning from data, knowledge is that meaning in a wider context. In social research data can be survey returns, diaries, interview transcripts, observation records and so on but in systematic review the data can be the papers that are collected and analysed.
Decolonising methodology	decolonisers are interested in critiquing dominant culture, in particular in relation to race, gender and sexual politics. They put the question of power centre stage, asking for example how research may be distorted by dominant interests of the coloniser and seek out alternative visions of, in our case, technology use. This often makes decolonisers action-oriented and seeking social justice.
Deduction	a top-down approach to inquiry which generally involves the testing of a formal hypothesis in experimental-type conditions, though deductive may be used in a looser sense of working from initial premises.
Descriptive statistics	this involves summarising the data in terms of variances, central tendencies, frequencies and so on.

Calculations include mean, mode, range, standard deviation, frequency tables. *Inferential statistics* make inferences about the wider population from the sample data, for example, calculations such as chi-square and t-Test.

Determinism a belief that human behaviour is the result of external factors, rather than as generated by internal motivation and intention.

Digital natives strongly contested idea in Prensky that young people were characterised by a preference for networking, quick processing of receiving information, multi-tasking, images over text. Digital natives were contrasted with *digital immigrants*, that is, older people (including teachers) who prefer step-by-step logic, and instructional strategies.

Digital tools refer to the hardware, software and electronic resources used in both formal and informal setting and as such may cover devices such as tablets, IWB, desktop computers and apps as well as content hosted in VLEs and websites. Digital tools took over from ICT as a favoured term.

E-learning (and M-learning and D-learning) definitions are disputed but e-learning was more associated with the use of digital tools in the context of distance learning, or at least learning without active teacher presence. M-learning was introduced to focus on a new wave of digital tools which were mobile and accessed wirelessly. Digital or D-learning is sometimes used to offer a more general definition, that is, any type of learning that is facilitated by technology.

Empirical research first-hand data collection through, say, interviewing, observation, questionnaire survey. It can be contrasted with desk research.

Epistemology how we come to know and understand the world. In social research there has long been debate about positivism and interpretivist epistemologies. *Positivism* seeks to carry out social *science* by drawing on experimental procedures established in natural science while *interpretivism* sees social *research* as having a special concern for uncovering the meaning people put on events. There is increasing interest in approaches which aim to bridge the gap between positivism and interpretivism.

Ethics   concern the moral principles guiding conduct, which may be held by a group or even a profession. In social research ethical issues often concern respect shown to others, the purpose of the research, who the research benefits and how it is reported. In this book ethics is raised in the context of online surveillance.

Experimental method (also 'scientific' method)   seeks to investigate, in a controlled context, the impact of one variable on another as measured by observable outcomes. Normally involves hypothesis testing, measurement of outcomes and hence comparison of control and experimental groups, that is, the experimental group are the people who experience the treatment or intervention, the control group are the people who do not.

Explanation   giving reasons why something happened. A positivist explanation is more likely to state cause and effect, may well use statistical testing of some kind, and see validity and reliability as 'warrants' of its quality. An interpretivist explanation is more concerned with uncovering the meaning of a phenomenon for those taking part as well as uncovering the consequences of their behaviour.

Face-to-face   interaction that involves two or more people who are physically present. Thus classroom learning and one to one mentoring are examples of F2F interaction. Remote teaching, for example, via Zoom or Teams, may be described as F2F as well, in order to stress that it is immediate and involves non-verbal communication.

Flipped classroom   a blended learning approach in which learners cover the content at home, for example, reviewing material within an VLE, and discussing it when they meet F2F, perhaps using group work within a problem-based learning approach.

Generalisability the extent to which it is feasible to use what was learnt in one context and apply it in another context. In the positivist tradition researchers assume generalisability but may end up making probabilistic statements, that is, by doing X and avoiding Y it is likely that some benefit will accrue.

Grounded theory is an inductive – or bottom-up – approach to theory generation. Grounded theory makes a virtue of beginning research with an open mind. The approach involves collecting data and organising it into codes, later themes and categories. It is theoretical in that it seeks to clarify, and at times model, the relationships between the categories which the researcher has generated.

Head mounted display (HMD) a display device attached to your head. Typically allows a mix of media and provides 360° vision. Navigation is often achieved through body, head or eye movement. Sometimes referred to as a 'Virtual Reality headset'.

Hybridity the idea that we are increasingly online and offline *at the same time*.

Induction drawing conclusions from many individual instances or observations. A bottom–up approach in its purist form is represented in grounded theory.

Information communication technology (ICT) generally refers to the use of electronic hardware and software and associated learning material. It was sometimes used more broadly to include analogue technology (for example, television, tape recorders and radio). ICT came to be used in preference to IT in educational sectors to put greater emphasis on communication and the role of interaction in teaching and learning.

Information technology (IT) the use of computers to create, process, store, retrieve and exchange all kinds of electronic data and information. IT is typically used within commercial rather than educational contexts in which the terms ICT and increasingly digital tools are preferred.

Interactive whiteboard (IWB) a large digital screen connected to a projector and a computer. Often in practice used for display only, using keyboard control. However, IWBs were designed to encourage annotation and navigation using digital pens, or finger movement on the screen. Board work can be saved and shared.

Learning analytics refers to the collection, analysis, and reporting of data about learners for purposes of supporting learning. A typical example includes analysis of automatically collected data about messages sent and messages viewed within a VLE.

Learning style a recognition that learners may orient themselves to a topic in preferred way (for example, deep, strategic and surface orientations to learning). In its stronger form a learning style is seen as an inherent preference for a certain way of learning across contexts, for example, an invariable preference for pictures over text.

Learning theory offers a description as to how students receive, process and retain knowledge during learning. Often described in terms of behaviourist, cognitivist and social constructivist learning theory.

Live online classes synchronous teaching events with students and teachers meeting in online rooms, typically using software such as Zoom, Teams and in synchronous spaces within a VLE. Presence is shown though video and voice (though with options to 'mute' both). Live classes generally have break out rooms, live 'chat' areas, screen sharing for presentations and feedback plus a 'whiteboard' or other tools for brainstorming.

Media in the context of technology studies media are the forms in which communication is carried out, for example text, pictures, audio and video. These categories can be worked, say to distinguish between digital/non-digital media; linear/interactive media; single media/multimedia and so on.

Method   the means through which data are gathered, for example interviewing, surveying, observing. Quantitative methods deal with the collecting and measuring of data in countable form, for example test scores, Likert scales, reaction times and so on. Qualitative methods involve collecting data in the form of text, images, film. In practice many studies will employ a mix of methods.

Methodology   in social research the methods, design and procedures within a study.

Mobile learning   learning that is enabled using mobile devices such as tablets and mobile phones. Mobile learning is seen as offering greater convenience and just in time access.

Model   modelling involves abstracting out in order to make a phenomenon clearer; a model highlights the most important factors or variables, and the ways in which they interact. A model might be a formula, a network analysis or other diagram, a concept, an ideal type and so on.

Normative   in philosophy associated with what ought to be the case rather than what is the case; normative social research is not and does not intend to be value-free. Social research may also set out to describe normative values held by those being researched.

Online   origins of the word are disputed but it was first used to describe a computer that was connected to another device but became later to refer to users connected to the internet, typically using Wi-Fi connection via a wireless router.

Ontology   in social research beliefs about the fundamental nature of reality, in particular social reality. Often discussed in terms of dichotomy between a belief in an objective reality, which exists independent of the observer, and reality as it appears subjectively or, more commonly, as negotiated within groups. There is increasing interest in approaches that mix ontological positions, for example, a belief in an objective reality, coupled with an understanding that reality can only be subjectively perceived.

Paradigms the dominant framework in which research takes places. This framework defines how problems are identified (what is to be studied); the epistemological and methodological assumptions behind the research (how it is to be studied); and what is done with the research (the nature and value of the knowledge generated).

Parsimony the principle of parsimony, also called Occam's razor, maintains that researchers should apply the simplest explanation possible to any set of observations.

Positionality how research might be affected by the researcher's own particular background, beliefs and values. Having a position is inevitable but it becomes a more sensitive issue when there is a great deal of asymmetry, for example, between the researcher and the researched, or, on a wider scale the difference in resources available to researchers in the global south and global north.

Problem-based learning an approach which sets students scenarios or problems which they work together to address. The community of inquiry model is a kind of problem-solving approach involving: *trigger* questions; *exploration* of solutions; *integration* of ideas; *resolution* of the problem. Different approaches to problem-based learning call for different levels of teacher involvement and cooperation.

Reification in social constructionism an institution or practice becomes reified when it takes on an independent existence, when it is taken for granted; in community of practice reification is described more neutrally as the products and processes which members of a community develop together.

Relatability
'able to connect with', for example readers may find a research study relatable if they are able to compare the case in the study with their own. Relatability is an alternative to generalisability and carries the idea of 'being able to learn from'.

Science and Technology Studies (STS)
an interdisciplinary field interested in the design and development of technology artefacts. It became more associated with the sociology of technology and the idea of actor networks and related approaches.

Self-organised learning
the idea of learning without, or with minimal, teacher intervention; learners are seen as producing order in an apparently chaotic situation.

Surveillance
the monitoring of activities, including individual behaviour, for the purpose of influencing or even controlling others.

Synchronous
happening at the same time, for example a conversation over Zoom. In contrast, asynchronous exchanges take place over time, for example, an email exchange over a period of days.

Systematic review
this weighs up the evidence from the literature using pre-determined criteria for inclusion and analysis. A meta-analysis can be considered as a particular kind of systematic review which seeks to aggregate outcomes in a quantitative fashion.

Technocentrism
a focus on the use of technology to solve educational problems and a belief that technology use is largely predictable.

Theorising
this is what you do when you make a theory. Theorising involves stepping back from the detail of a study and looking at how each observation might be linked up. Theorising is a leap of the imagination, but it is not about making things

up, the imagination is constrained by what the data allow and framed by ideas from the past. In theorising researchers are thinking about the bigger picture and that makes theorising difficult.

Theory here an inclusive term to capture different ways of providing an explanation for a phenomenon. Theory abstracts out what is important in order to make complicated scenarios comprehensible to an audience. Theories generated in one context are useable or at least relatable to other researchers.

Tool this is usually understood as physical object designed for achieving tasks, for example, a hammer is a tool for banging in nails, though tools can be put to purposes for which they were not designed. The term has transferred into ICT studies to include both software such as word processor, presentation programmes, spreadsheets, and hardware such as mobile phone, tablet, radio. Vygotsky and others sometimes describe language as a tool in that it enables thought.

Unplugging literally to live temporarily without computer-related devices, typically in order to take stock of habits of use and to better focus on physical interactions and well-being.

Virtual learning environment (VLE) a programme which contains a mix of functions including: storage of material (for example, presentations and tutorials); forums; multiple-choice and quiz software; administration of registers, assessment and outcome data; synchronous or 'live' classes; access to an e-library. A VLE is typically contained within the one system (for example, Moodle or Blackboard) but the same functionality can be achieved with a mix of software, this is often referred to as a learning platform.

Virtual reality (VR) describes a perception of being physically present in a non-physical world. The perception is created by surrounding the user with images, sound or other stimuli. VR applications are typically interactive and may involve headsets. Immersive reality offers something similar but without the use of headsets.

Augmented reality uses digital technology to alter the physical world, for example, Pokémon game players used their mobile phones to find Pokémon overlaid on the physical environment.

Web 1.0/Web 2.0/
Web 3.0

these are terms sometimes used in education research but more associated with the IT industry. There are competing definitions but Web 1.0 refers to the earlier days of the Internet (up to around 2004) in which the focus was on viewing content including personal web pages and blogs. Web 2.0 brought networking into the mainstream and covered the rise of user-created, interactive social networking sites such as Myspace and Facebook. Web 3.0 has much in common with Web 2.0 but here there is a more explicit focus on user-generated activity and alternatives to 'Big Tech'. This sounds more democratic but has generated concerns over harmful content and security. Crypto currencies are associated with Web 3.0. Some talk about Web 4.0 to draw attention to artificial intelligence, while Web 5.0 is/will be about the constant (emotional) interaction between humans and computers.

References

Abend, G. (2008). The meaning of 'theory'. *Sociological Theory*, 26(2), 173–199.

Aggeliki, T., Komis, V. and Karsenti, K. (2018). A methodological framework for investigating TPACK integration in educational activities using ICT by prospective early childhood teachers. *Italian Journal of Educational Technology*, 26(1), 71–89.

Agudo-Peregrina, Á.F., Iglesias-Pradas, S., Conde-González, M.Á. and Hernández-García, Á. (2014). Can we predict success from log data in VLEs? Classification of interactions for learning analytics and their relation with performance in VLE-supported F2F and online learning. *Computers in Human Behavior*, 31, 542–550.

Akçayır, G. and Akçayır, M. (2018). The flipped classroom: A review of its advantages and challenges. *Computers & Education*, 126, 334–345.

Altenried, M. (2020). The platform as factory: Crowdwork and the hidden labour behind artificial intelligence. *Capital & Class*, 44(2), 145–158.

Amichai-Hamburger, Y., Gazit, T., Bar-Ilan, J., Perez, O., Aharony, N., Bronstein, J. and Dyne, T.S. (2016). Psychological factors behind the lack of participation in online discussions. *Computers in Human Behavior*, 55, 268–277.

Anderson, B. (2016). Frameworks of comparison. *London Review of Books*, 38(2), 15–18.

Arendt, H. (1961). The crisis in education. In H. Arendt, *Between past and present* (pp 173–196). Viking Press.

Arnott, L., Palaiologou, I. and Gray, C. (2019). Internet of toys across home and early childhood education: Understanding the ecology of the child's social world. *Technology, Pedagogy and Education*, 28(4), 401–412.

Baker, T., Tricarico, L. and Bielli, S. (2019). Making the most of technology in education NESTA/NESTA Italia. [Online], https://www.nesta.org.uk/report/making-most-technology-education/

Ball, D. (1990). What is the role of IT within the National Mathematics Curriculum? *Journal of Computer Assisted Learning*, 6(4), 239–245.

Banerjee, A.V., Cole, S., Duflo, E. and Linden, L. (2007). Remedying education: Evidence from two randomized experiments in India. *The Quarterly Journal of Economics*, 122(3), 1235–1264.

Barnett, R. (1994). *The limits of competence: Knowledge, higher education and society*. Open University Press.

Basak, S. K., Wotto, M. and Bélanger, P. (2018). E-learning, M-learning and D-learning: Conceptual definition and comparative analysis. *Learning and Digital Media*, 15(4), 191–216.

Batane, T. and Ngwako, A. (2017). Factors influencing school management teams in implementing ICT policy in Botswana schools. *Australasian Journal of Educational Technology*, 33(1). [Online], https://ajet.org.au/index.php/AJET/article/view/2299

Becker, H.J. (1994). How exemplary computer-using teachers differ from other teachers: Implications for realizing the potential of computers in schools. *Journal of Research on Computing in Education*, 26(3), 291–321.

Bentley, C.M., Nemer, D. and Vannini, S. (2019). 'When words become unclear': Unmasking ICT through visual methodologies in participatory ICT4D. *AI & Society*, 34(3), 477–549.

Berger, P. and Luckmann, T. (1966). *The social construction of reality: A treatise in the sociology of knowledge*. Anchor Books.

Bhagat, S., Jeong, E.J. and Kim, D.J. (2020). The role of individuals' need for online social interactions and interpersonal incompetence in digital game addiction. *International Journal of Human–Computer Interaction*, 36(5), 449–463.

Biesta, G. (2010). Why 'what works' still won't work: From evidence-based education to value-based education. *Studies in Philosophy and Education*, 29(5), 491–503.

Biesta, G., Allan, J. and Edwards, R. (2014). *Making a difference in theory*. Routledge.

Bigum, C. (1998). Solutions in search of educational problems: Speaking for computers in schools. *Educational Policy*, 12(5), 586–601.

Bijker, W. (1997). *Bicycles, Bakelites, and bulbs: Toward a theory of sociotechnical change*. MIT Press.

Blanton, M., Westbrook, S. and Carter, G. (2005). Using Valsiner's zone theory to interpret teaching practices in mathematics and science classrooms. *Journal of Mathematics Teacher Education*, 8(1), 5–33.

Blin, F. and Appel, C. (2011). Computer supported collaborative writing in practice: An activity theoretical study. *CALICO Journal*, 28(2), 473–497.

Blin, F. and Munro, M. (2008). Why hasn't technology disrupted academics' teaching practices? Understanding resistance to change through the lens of activity theory. *Computers & Education*, 50(2), 475–490.

Bourdieu, P. (1986). The forms of capital. In J. Richardson (ed), *Handbook of theory and research for the sociology of education* (pp 241–258). Greenwood.

boyd, d. (2014). *It's complicated: The social lives of networked teens*. Yale University Press.

Braun, V. and Clarke, V. (2019). *Thematic analysis: A practical guide*. SAGE.

Bronfenbrenner, U. (1979). *The ecology of human development*. Harvard University Press.

Bruner, J. (2020). *The culture of education*. Harvard University Press.

Buckingham, D. (2007a). *Beyond technology: Children's learning in the age of digital culture*. Polity.

Buckingham, D. (2007b). *Youth, identity, and digital media*. MIT Press.

Bulfin, S., Henderson, M. and Johnson, N. (2013). Examining the use of theory within educational technology and media research. *Learning, Media and Technology*, 38(3), 337–344.

Bulfin, S., Johnson, N. and Bigum, C. (2015). *Critical perspectives on technology and education.* Springer.

Bush, T. and Glover, D. (2014). School leadership models: What do we know? *School Leadership & Management,* 34(5), 553–571.

Carr, W. and Kemmis, S. (1986). *Becoming critical: Education, knowledge and action research.* Falmer.

Carson, R. (2018). *Rachel Carson: Silent spring and other writings on the environment,* edited by S. Steinberger. Library of America.

Centre for Education Research and Innovation (2008). *21st century learning: Research, innovation and policy directions from recent OECD analyses.* OECD.

Chan, C.K. and van Aalst, J. (2018). Knowledge building: Theory, design, and analysis. In F. Fischer, C.E. Hmelo-Silver, S.R. Goldman and P. Reimann (eds), *International handbook of the learning sciences* (pp 295–307). Routledge.

Chandler, D. (1983). *Young learners and the microcomputer.* Open University Press.

Chang, C.-H., Irvine, K., Wu, B.S. and Seow, T. (2018). Reflecting on field-based and technology-enabled learning in geography. In C.-H. Chang, B.S. Wu, T. Seow and K. Irvine (eds), *Learning geography beyond the traditional classroom* (pp 201–212). Springer.

Clay, C.A. (2011). Exploring the use of mobile technologies for the acquisition of clinical skills. *Nurse Education Today,* 31(6), 582–586.

Clegg, S. (2001). Theorising the machine: Gender, education and computing. *Gender and Education,* 13(3), 307–324.

Clegg, S. and Trayhurn, D. (2000). Gender and computing: Not the same old problem. *British Educational Research Journal,* 26(1), 75–89.

Cole, J., Nolan, J., Seko, Y., Mancuso, K. and Ospina, A. (2011). GimpGirl grows up: Women with disabilities rethinking, redefining, and reclaiming community. *New Media & Society,* 13(7), 1161–1179.

Cole, M. and Engeström, Y. (1993). A cultural-historic approach to distributed cognition. In G. Salomon (ed), *Distributed cognitions: Psychological and educational considerations* (pp 1–46). Cambridge University Press.

Colton, J. (2019). Breaking out, finding and using information: Theorising learner identities in assemblages of teaching and learning with technology. *Technology, Pedagogy and Education,* 28(4), 425–434.

Conole, G. and Dyke, M. (2004). What are the affordances of information and communication technologies? *Research in Learning Technology,* 12(2), 113–124.

Conwell, M.J. (1964). An evaluation of the Keating report. *The Bulletin of the National Association of Secondary School Principals,* 48(290), 104–115.

Coolican, H. (2019). *Research methods and statistics in psychology.* Routledge.

Costa, C. (2015). Academics online: Fighting for a new habitus. In C. Costa and M. Murphy (eds), *Bourdieu, habitus and social research* (pp 151–166). Springer.

Creswell, J.W. and Creswell, J.D. (2017). *Research design: Qualitative, quantitative, and mixed methods approaches.* SAGE.

Crotty, M. (1998). *The foundations of social research.* SAGE.

Cuban, L. (1986). *Teachers and machines: The classroom use of technology since 1920.* Teachers College Press.

Cuban, L. (2001). *Oversold and underused: Computers in the classroom.* Harvard University Press.

Cuban, L., Kirkpatrick, H. and Peck, C. (2001). High access and low use of technologies in high school classrooms: Explaining an apparent paradox. *American Educational Research Journal*, 38(4), 813–834.

Dablanc, L., Morganti, E., Arvidsson, N., Woxenius, J., Browne, M. and Saidi, N. (2017). The rise of on-demand 'Instant Deliveries' in European cities. *Supply Chain Forum: An International Journal*, 18(4), 203–217.

Darling-Hammond, L. and Oakes, J. (2021). *Preparing teachers for deeper learning.* Harvard Education Press.

Davis, F. (1989). Perceived usefulness, perceived ease of use, and user acceptance of information technology. *MIS Quarterly*, 13(3), 319–340.

Davis, F. and Venkatesh, V. (1996). A critical assessment of potential measurement biases in the technology acceptance model: Three experiments. *International Journal of Human-Computer Studies*, 45, 19–45.

Davis, N. (2017). *Digital technologies and change in education: The arena framework.* Routledge.

Davis, N., Harris, L. and Cunningham, U. (2019). Professional ecologies shaping technology adoption in early childhood education with multilingual children. *British Journal of Educational Technology*, 50(3), 1320–1339.

Day, C. (1999). *Developing teachers: The challenges of lifelong learning.* Falmer.

De Souza e Silva, A. (2006). From cyber to hybrid: Mobile technologies as interfaces of hybrid spaces. *Space and Culture*, 9(3), 261–278.

Dewey, J. (1916/1947). *Democracy and education.* The Macmillan Company.

Dimopoulos, K., Koutsampelas, C. and Tsatsaroni, A. (2021). Home schooling through online teaching in the era of COVID-19: Exploring the role of home-related factors that deepen educational inequalities across European societies. *European Educational Research Journal*, 20(4), 479–497.

Downes, T. (2002). Blending play, practice and performance: Children's use of the computer at home. *Journal of Educational Enquiry*, 3(2), 21–34.

Drachsler, H. and Schneider, J. (2018). JCAL special issue on multimodal learning analytics. *Journal of Computer Assisted Learning*, 34(4), 335–337.

Drew, C. and Mann, A. (2018). Unfitting, uncomfortable, unacademic: A sociological reading of an interactive mobile phone app in university lectures. *International Journal of Educational Technology in Higher Education*, 15(1), 1–13.

Driver, R. (2008). *The pupil as scientist?* Open University Press.

Eco, U. (2015). *How to write a thesis.* MIT Press.

Elkin, D. (2007). *The power of play: Learning what comes naturally.* Hachette.

Engeström, Y. (2001). Expansive learning at work: Toward an activity theoretical reconceptualization. *Journal of Education and Work*, 14(1), 133–156.

Ertmer, P. (2005). Teacher pedagogical beliefs: The final frontier in our quest for technology integration? *Educational Technology Research and Development*, 53(4), 25–39.

Evans, T. (2002). Part-time research students: Are they producing knowledge where it counts? *Higher Education Research and Development*, 21(2), 155–165.

Eyal, L. and Gil, E. (2022). Hybrid learning spaces: A three-fold evolving perspective. In *Hybrid learning spaces* (pp 11–23). Springer.

Fauske, J. and Wade, S. (2003). Research to practice online: Conditions that foster democracy, community, and critical thinking in computer-mediated discussions. *Journal of Research on Technology in Education*, 36(2), 137–153.

Feenberg, A. (2017). A critical theory of technology. In U. Felt, R. Fouché, C. Miller and L. Smith-Doerr (eds), *Handbook of science and technology studies* (pp 635–663). MIT Press.

Fianu, E., Blewett, C. and Ampong, G.O. (2020). Toward the development of a model of student usage of MOOCs. *Education + Training*, 62(5), 521–541.

Fishbein, M. and Ajzen, I. (1980). *Understanding social attitudes and predicting social behaviour.* Prentice Hall.

Fukuyama, F. (2011). *The great disruption: Human nature and the reconstitution of social order.* Humanitas Press.

Fullan, M. (2007). *The new meaning of educational change* (4th edn). Teachers College Press.

Fullan, M. and Langworthy, M. (2013). *Towards a new end: New pedagogies for deep learning.* Creative Commons.

Garrison, D.R., Anderson, T. and Archer, W. (2001). Critical thinking, cognitive presence, and computer conferencing in distance education. *American Journal of Distance Education*, 15(1), 7–23.

Gee, J. (2005). Semiotic social spaces and affinity spaces. In D. Barton and K. Tusting (eds), *Beyond communities of practice: Language power and social context* (pp 214–232). Cambridge University Press.

Gee, J. (2018). Affinity spaces: How young people live and learn on line and out of school. *Phi Delta Kappan*, 99(6), 8–13.

Giattino, C., Ortiz-Ospina, E. and Roser, M. (2020). Working hours. [Online], https://ourworldindata.org/working-hours

Gibson, J. (1986). *The ecological approach to visual perception.* Lawrence Erlbaum Associates.

Giddens, A. (1990). *The consequences of modernity.* Polity.

Glaser, B. and Strauss, A. (1967). *The discovery of grounded theory: Strategies for qualitative research.* Sociology Press.

Goethe, J.W. (2016) *Maximen und Reflexionen.* Holzing.

Goldman, S. and Scardamalia, M. (2013). Managing, understanding, applying, and creating knowledge in the information age: Next-generation challenges and opportunities. *Cognition and Instruction*, 31(2), 255–269.

Goos, M. (2005). A sociocultural analysis of the development of pre-service and beginning teachers' pedagogical identities as users of technology. *Journal of Mathematics Teacher Education*, 8(1), 35–59.

Greenfield, S. (2015). *Mind change: How digital technologies are leaving their mark on our brains*. Random House.

Grenfell, M. (2004). *Pierre Bourdieu: Agent provocateur*. Continuum.

Gunawardena, C., Lowe, C. and Anderson, T. (1997). Analysis of a global online debate and the development of an interaction analysis model for examining social construction of knowledge in computer conferencing. *Journal of Educational Computing Research*, 17(4), 397–431.

Hall, E. and Moseley, D. (2005). Is there a role for learning styles in personalised education and training? *International Journal of Lifelong Education*, 24(3), 243–255.

Hamilton, D., McKechnie, J., Edgerton, E. and Wilson, C. (2021). Immersive virtual reality as a pedagogical tool in education: A systematic literature review of quantitative learning outcomes and experimental design. *Journal of Computers in Education*, 8(1), 1–32.

Hammond, M. (2010). What is an affordance and can it help us understand the use of ICT in education? *Education and Information Technologies*, 15(3), 205–217.

Hammond, M. (2013). The contribution of pragmatism to understanding educational action research: Value and consequences. *Educational Action Research*, 21(4), 603–661.

Hammond, M. (2018). 'An interesting paper but not sufficiently theoretical': What does theorising in social research look like? *Methodological Innovations*, May–August, 1–10.

Hammond, M. (2022). *Writing a postgraduate thesis or dissertation*. Routledge.

Hammond, M. and Alotaibi, B. (2017). Theorising the take-up of ICT: Can Valsiner's three zones framework make a contribution? *Technology, Pedagogy and Education*, 26(2), 139–155.

Hammond, M. and Wellington, J. (2019). *Education research: The basics*. Routledge.

Hammond, M. and Wellington, J. (2021). *Research methods: The key concepts*. Routledge.

Hargreaves, A. (2001). *Changing teachers, changing times: Teachers' work and culture in the postmodern age*. Teachers College Press.

Hasan, M. (2016). Positivism: To what extent does it aid our understanding of the contemporary social world? *Quality & Quantity*, 50(1), 317–325.

Hattie, J. (2013). *Visible learning: A synthesis of over 800 meta-analyses relating to achievement*. Routledge.

Haythornthwaite, C., de Laat, M. and Dawson, S. (2013). Introduction to the special issue on learning analytics. *American Behavioral Scientist*, 57(10), 1371–1379.

Hennekam, S., Macarthur, S., Bennett, D., Hope, C. and Goh, T. (2020). Women composers' use of online communities of practice to build and support their careers. *Personnel Review*, 49(1), 215–230.

Hennessy, S., Harrison, D. and Wamakote, L. (2010). Teacher factors influencing classroom use of ICT in sub-Saharan Africa. *Itupale Online Journal of African Studies*, 2(1), 39–54.

Henri, F. (1992). Computer conferencing and content analysis. In A. Kaye (ed), *Collaborative learning through computer conferencing* (pp 117–136). Springer.

Hickman, L. (2009). John Dewey as a philosopher of technology. In D. Kaplan (ed), *Readings in the philosophy of technology* (pp 43–55). Rowman & Littlefield.

Higgins, S. (2018). *Improving learning: Meta-analysis of intervention research in education*. Cambridge University Press.

Higgins, S., Xiao, Z. and Katsipataki, M. (2012). *The impact of digital technology on learning: A summary for the education endowment foundation*. Full report. Education Endowment Foundation.

Hirsch Jr, E.D. (2010). *The schools we need: And why we don't have them*. Anchor.

Hirst, P. (1965). Educational theory. In J. Tibbles (ed), *The study of education* (pp 29–58). Routledge and Kegan Paul.

Hjortshoj, K. (2018). *From student to scholar: A guide to writing through the dissertation stage*. Routledge.

Hobsbawm, E.J. (1999). *Industry and empire: From 1750 to the present day*. The New Press.

Hodkinson, P. and Hodkinson, H. (2003). Individuals, communities of practice and the policy context: School teachers' learning in their workplace. *Studies in Continuing Education*, 25(1), 3–21.

Howard, D. and Giovanelli, M. (2019). Einstein's philosophy of science. In E.N. Zalta (ed), *The Stanford encyclopedia of philosophy*. [Online], https://plato.stanford.edu/entries/einstein-philscience/

Hung, J.-L., Shelton, B.E., Yang, J. and Du, X. (2019). Improving predictive modeling for at-risk student identification: A multistage approach. *IEEE Transactions on Learning Technologies*, 12(2), 148–157.

Illeris, K. (2018). An overview of the history of learning theory. *European Journal of Education*, 53(1), 86–101.

Illich, I. (1973). *Deschooling society*. Penguin.

Inel Ekici, D. (2018). Development of pre-service teachers' teaching self-efficacy beliefs through an online community of practice. *Asia Pacific Education Review*, 19(1), 27–40.

Jackson, B. (2019). Doomed to draw. *London Review of Books*, 41(11), 34–36.

Jadán-Guerrero, J., Guevara, C., Lara-Alvarez, P., Sanchez-Gordon, S., Calle-Jimenez, T., Salvador-Ullauri, L., Acosta-Vargas, P. and Bonilla-Jurado, D. (2020). Building hybrid interfaces to increase interaction with young children and children with special needs. In I. Nunes (ed), *Advances in human factors and systems interaction* (pp 306–314). Springer.

Jamieson-Proctor, R.M., Burnett, P.C., Finger, G. and Watson, G. (2006). ICT integration and teachers' confidence in using ICT for teaching and learning in Queensland state schools. *Australasian Journal of Educational Technology*, 22(4), 511–530.

Johannesen, M. and Habib, L. (2010). The role of professional identity in patterns of use of multiple-choice assessment tools. *Technology, Pedagogy and Education*, 19(1), 93–109.

John, P. (2005). The sacred and the profane: Subject sub-culture, pedagogical practice and teachers' perceptions of the classroom uses of ICT. *Educational Review*, 57(4), 471–490.

Johnson, D. and Johnson, R. (1989). *Cooperation and competition: Theory and research*. Interaction Book Company.

Johnson, D., Johnson, R. and Smith, K. (1998). Cooperative learning returns to college: What evidence is there that it works? *Change: The Magazine of Higher Learning*, 30(4), 26–35.

Johnson, N.F. (2019). Dysfunctional devices in the classroom meet the habitus of the new. *E-learning and Digital Media*, 16(3), 208–220.

Jones, C. (2015). *Networked learning: An educational paradigm for the age of digital networks*. Springer International Publishing.

Jovanović, J., Saqr, M., Joksimović, S. and Gašević, D. (2021). Students matter the most in learning analytics: The effects of internal and instructional conditions in predicting academic success. *Computers & Education*, 172, 104251.

Kang, X. and Zhang, W. (2020). An experimental case study on forum-based online teaching to improve student's engagement and motivation in higher education. *Interactive Learning Environments*, 1–12.

Kassab, M., DeFranco, J. and Laplante, P. (2020). A systematic literature review on internet of things in education: Benefits and challenges. *Journal of Computer Assisted Learning*, 36(2), 115–127.

Keating, R.F. (1963). *A study of the effectiveness of language laboratories: A preliminary evaluation in twenty-one school systems of the metropolitan school study council*. Columbia University.

Keith, T.Z. (2019). *Multiple regression and beyond: An introduction to multiple regression and structural equation modeling*. Routledge.

Kendall, G. (2019). Would your mobile phone be powerful enough to get you to the moon? *The Conversation*. [Online], https://theconversation.com/would-your-mobile-phone-be-powerful-enough-to-get-you-to-the-moon-115933

Khlaif, Z.N., Salha, S. and Kouraichi, B. (2021). Emergency remote learning during COVID-19 crisis: Students' engagement. *Education and Information Technologies*, 26(6), 7033–7055.

Kiley, M. (2015). 'I didn't have a clue what they were talking about': PhD candidates and theory. *Innovations in Education and Teaching International*, 52(1), 52–63.

Klein, G., Suvin, D. and Lecorps, L. (1977). Discontent in American science fiction. *Science Fiction Studies*, 4(1), 3–13.

Krause, M. (2016). The meanings of theorizing. *The British Journal of Sociology*, 67(1), 23–29.

Kuhn, T. (2012/1962). *The structure of scientific revolutions*. University of Chicago Press.

Kumpulainen, K. and Sefton-Green, J. (2014). What is connected learning and how to research it? *International Journal of Learning and Media*, 4(2), 7–18.

Kwet, M. (2017). Operation Phakisa Education: Why a secret? Mass surveillance, inequality, and race in South Africa's emerging national e-education system. *First Monday*, 22(12). [Online], https://doi.org/10.5210/fm.v22i12.8054

Latour, B. (1999). *Pandora's hope: Essays on the reality of science studies*. Harvard University Press.

Latour, B. (2002). Morality and technology, the end of the means. *Theory, Culture and Society*, 19(5/6), 247–260 (translated by C. Venn).

Laurillard, D. (1993). *Rethinking university teaching: A framework for the effective use of educational technology*. Routledge.

Lave, J. (1977). Cognitive consequences of traditional apprenticeship training in West Africa. *Anthropology & Education Quarterly*, 8(3), 177–180.

Lave, J. and Wenger, E. (1991). *Situated learning: Legitimate peripheral participation*. Cambridge University Press.

Lazem, S., Giglitto, D., Nkwo, M.S., Mthoko, H., Upani, J. and Peters, A. (2021). Challenges and paradoxes in decolonising HCI: A critical discussion. *Computer Supported Cooperative Work*, 31(2), 159–196.

Lear, L. (2009). *Witness for nature*. Houghton, Mifflin and Harcourt.

Leask, M. and Younie, S. (2021). *Ensuring schooling for all in times of crisis: Lessons from Covid-19*. Routledge.

Leithwood, K., Harris, A. and Hopkins, D. (2008). Seven strong claims about successful school leadership. *School Leadership and Management*, 28(1), 27–42.

Leu, D., Kinzer, C., Coiro, J. and Cammack, D. (2004). Toward a theory of new literacies emerging from the internet and other information and communication technologies. *Theoretical Models and Processes of Reading*, 5(1), 1570–1613.

Levin, T. and Wadmany, R. (2005). Changes in educational beliefs and classroom practices of teachers and students in rich technology-based classrooms. *Technology, Pedagogy and Education*, 14(3), 281–307.

Lim, C.P., Ra, S., Chin, B. and Wang, T. (2020). Information and communication technologies (ICT) for access to quality education in the global south: A case study of Sri Lanka. *Education and Information Technologies*, 25(4), 2447–2462.

Lindtner, S., Nardi, B., Wang, Y., Mainwaring, S., Jing, H. and Liang, W. (2008). A hybrid cultural ecology: World of warcraft in China. Paper presented at the Proceedings of the 2008 ACM conference on Computer Supported Cooperative Work, 8–12 November, San Diego.

Livingstone, S. and Sefton-Green, J. (2016). *The class: Living and learning in the digital age*. New York University Press.

Lyon, D. (2019). Surveillance capitalism, surveillance culture and data politics. In D. Bigo, I. Isin and E. Ruppert (eds), *Data politics* (pp 64–77). Routledge.

MacDonald, B. (1977). The educational evaluation of NDPCAL. *British Journal of Educational Technology*, 8(3), 176–189.

MacKenzie, D. and Wajcman, J. (1999). *The social shaping of technology*. Open University Press.

Magnifico, A., Lammers, J. and Fields, D. (2018). Affinity spaces, literacies and classrooms: Tensions and opportunities. *Literacy*, 52(3), 145–152.

Mama, M. and Hennessy, S. (2013). Developing a typology of teacher beliefs and practices concerning classroom use of ICT. *Computers & Education*, 68, 380–387.

Marcuse, H. (2013/1964). *One-dimensional man: Studies in the ideology of advanced industrial society*. Routledge.

Martin, T. and Sherin, B. (2013). Learning analytics and computational techniques for detecting and evaluating patterns in learning: An introduction to the special issue. *Journal of the Learning Sciences*, 22(4), 511–520.

Martindale, D. (2013). *The nature and types of sociological theory* (vol 11). Routledge.

Mavri, A., Ioannou, A. and Loizides, F. (2020). Design students meet industry players: Feedback and creativity in communities of practice. *Thinking Skills and Creativity*, 37, 100684.

McNiff, J. (2017). *Action research: All you need to know*. SAGE.

McQuaide, S. (2009). Making education equitable in rural China through distance learning. *The International Review of Research in Open and Distributed Learning*, 10(1).

Medawar, P. (1963). Is the scientific paper a fraud? *The Listener*, 70(September), 377–378.

Mei, S., Hu, Y., Wu, X., Cao, R., Kong, Y., Zhang, L., Lin, X., Hu, Y. and Li, L. (2022). Health risks of mobile phone addiction among college students in China. *International Journal of Mental Health and Addiction*, 1–16.

Miles, M.B., Huberman, A.M. and Saldana, J. (2013). *Qualitative data analysis: A methods sourcebook*. SAGE.

Miller, R. (2011). *Vygotsky in perspective*. Cambridge University Press.

Mills, C.W. (1959). *The sociological imagination*. Oxford University Press.

Mishra, P. and Koehler, M. (2006). Technological pedagogical content knowledge: A framework for teacher knowledge. *Teachers College Record*, 108(6), 1017–1054.

Mitra, S., Kulkarni, S. and Stanfield, J. (2016). Learning at the edge of chaos: Self-organising systems in education. In H. Lees and N. Noddings (eds), *The Palgrave international handbook of alternative education* (pp 227–239). Palgrave Macmillan.

Mogas, J., Palau, R., Fuentes, M. and Cebrián, G. (2022). Smart schools on the way: How school principals from Catalonia approach the future of education within the fourth industrial revolution. *Learning Environments Research*, 25, 875–893.

Morris, N. and Cravens Pickens, J.D. (2017). 'I'm not a gadget': A grounded theory on unplugging. *The American Journal of Family Therapy*, 45(5), 264–282.

Morze, N.V. and Glazunova, O.G. (2014). Design of electronic learning courses for it students considering the dominant learning style. In V. Ermolayev, H.C. Mayr, M. Nikitchenko, A. Spivakovsky and G. Zholtkevych (eds), *Information and communication technologies in education, research, and industrial applications* (pp 261–273). Springer.

Nardi, P.M. (2018). *Doing survey research: A guide to quantitative methods*. Routledge.

Nerland, M. and Jensen, K. (2010). Objectual practice and learning in professional work. In S. Billett (ed), *Learning through practice: Models, traditions, orientations and approaches* (pp 82–103). Springer.

Ng, W.L., Teo, B.C., Yeo, J.B., Ho, W.K. and Teo, K.M. (2019). Use of technology in mathematics education. In *Mathematics education in Singapore* (pp 313–348). Springer.

Nikolaidou, G. (2012). ComPLuS model: A new insight in pupils' collaborative talk, actions and balance during a computer-mediated music task. *Computers & Education*, 58(2), 740–765.

Norman, D. (2013). *The design of everyday things* (revised and expanded edn). Basic Books.

OECD. (2015). *Students, computers and learning: Making the connection*. OECD.

OECD. (2017). *The OECD handbook for innovative learning environments, educational research and innovation*. OECD.

Oliver, M. (2011). Technological determinism in educational technology research: Some alternative ways of thinking about the relationship between learning and technology. *Journal of Computer Assisted Learning*, 27(5), 373–384.

Olson, J. (1988). *Schoolworlds/microworlds: Computers and the culture of the school*. Pergamon.

Papert, S. (1980). *Mindstorms: Children, computers and powerful ideas*. Basic Books.

Papert, S. (1993). *Children's machine: Rethinking school in the age of the computer*. Basic Books.

Passey, D. (2013). *Inclusive technology enhanced learning: Overcoming cognitive, physical, emotional, and geographic challenges*. Routledge.

Perkins, D. (1993). Person-plus: A distributed view of thinking and learning. In G. Salomon (ed), *Distributed cognitions: Psychological and educational considerations* (pp 88–110). Cambridge University Press.

Petko, D., Prasse, D. and Cantieni, A. (2018). The interplay of school readiness and teacher readiness for educational technology integration: A structural equation model. *Computers in the Schools*, 35(1), 1–18.

Pitura, J. and Terlecka-Pacut, E. (2018). Action research on the application of technology assisted urban gaming in language education in a Polish upper-secondary school. *Computer Assisted Language Learning*, 31(7), 734–763.

Polanyi, M. (1958). *Personal knowledge: Towards a post-critical philosophy*. University of Chicago Press.

Pradhan, V. and Hyde, L. (2022). The use of technology to support remote teaching and learning during the Covid-19 pandemic: Responses in South Asia. In M. Hammond (ed), *Supporting remote teaching and learning in developing countries: From the global to the local* (pp 3–5). British Council: Nepal.

Prensky, M. (2001). Digital natives, digital immigrants. *On the Horizon*, 9(5), 1–6.

Prout, A. (1996). Actor-network theory, technology and medical sociology: An illustrative analysis of the metered dose inhaler. *Sociology of Health & Illness*, 18(2), 198–219.

Punch, K. (2009). *Introduction to research methods in education*. SAGE.

Rana, K., Greenwood, J. and Fox-Turnbull, W. (2020). Implementation of Nepal's education policy in ICT: Examining current practice through an ecological model. *The Electronic Journal of Information Systems in Developing Countries*, 86(2), e12118.

Razzouk, R. and Shute, V. (2012). What is design thinking and why is it important? *Review of Educational Research*, 82(3), 330–348.

Reese, W. (2001). The origins of progressive education. *History of Education Quarterly*, 41(2), 1–24.

Rheingold, H. (1993). *The virtual community: Homesteading on the electronic frontier*. MIT Press.

Robins, K. and Webster, F. (1988). Athens without slaves … or slaves without Athens? The neurosis of technology. *Science as Culture*, 1(3), 7–53.

Robson, C. and McCartan, K. (2016). *Real world research*. John Wiley & Sons.

Rogers, E.M. (2010). *Diffusion of innovations*. Simon & Schuster.

Ryan, A. (1995). *John Dewey and the high tide of American liberalism*. W.W. Norton and Company.

Sadaf, A., Newby, T.J. and Ertmer, P.A. (2016). An investigation of the factors that influence preservice teachers' intentions and integration of Web 2.0 tools. *Educational Technology Research and Development*, 64(1), 37–64.

Salmon, G., Nie, M. and Edirisingha, P. (2010). Developing a five-stage model of learning in Second Life. *Educational Research*, 52(2), 169–182.

Salomon, G.E. (1993). *Distributed cognitions: Psychological and educational considerations.* Cambridge University Press.

Sang, G., Valcke, M., Braak, J.V. and Tondeur, J. (2010). Student teachers' thinking processes and ICT integration: Predictors of prospective teaching behaviors with educational technology. *Computers & Education*, 54(1), 103–112.

Scardamalia, M. and Bereiter, C. (2003). Knowledge building. In J. W. Guthrie (ed), *Encyclopedia of education* (pp 1370–1373). Macmillan Reference.

Scardamalia, M. and Bereiter, C. (2006). Knowledge building: Theory, pedagogy, and technology. In K. Sawyer (ed), *Cambridge handbook of the learning sciences* (pp 97–118). Cambridge University Press.

Schramm, W. (1962). Learning from instructional television. *Review of Educational Research*, 32(2), 156–167.

Sellar, S., Thompson, G. and Rutkowski, D. (2017). *The global education race: Taking the measure of PISA and international testing.* Brush Education.

Selwyn, N. (2011a). Editorial: In praise of pessimism—the need for negativity in educational technology. *British Journal of Educational Technology*, 42(5), 713–718.

Selwyn, N. (2011b). Making sense of young people, education and digital technology: The role of sociological theory. *Oxford Review of Education*, 38(1), 81–96.

Shakespeare, W. (1598/1997). *As you like it.* [Online], https://www.gutenb erg.org/ebooks/1121

Shrader-Frechette, K. and Westra, L. (1997). *Technology and values.* Rowman & Littlefield.

Shulman, L.S. (1986). Those who understand: Knowledge growth in teaching. *Educational Researcher*, 15(4), 4–14.

Siemens, G. (2005). Connectivism: A learning theory for the digital age. *International Journal of Instructional Technology and Distance Learning*, 2(1), 3–10.

Siyahhan, S., Barab, S.A. and Downton, M.P. (2010). Using activity theory to understand intergenerational play: The case of Family Quest. *International Journal of Computer-Supported Collaborative Learning*, 5(4), 415–432.

Skinner, B. (1953). *Science and human behavior.* Macmillan

Smahel, D., Machackova, H., Mascheroni, G., Dedkova, L., Staksrud, E., Ólafsson, K., Livingstone, S. and Hasebrink, U. (2020). *EU kids online 2020: Survey results from 19 countries.* LSE.

SMART (nd). *School in a bag.* [Online], https://smart.com.ph/About/lea rnsmart/programs-projects/school-in-a-bag

Smith, F. (1988). *Joining the literacy club: Further essays into education.* Heinemann Educational Publishers.

Spillane, J.P. (2005). Distributed leadership. *The Educational Forum*, 69, 143–150.

Stahl, G., Koschmann, T. and Suthers, D. (2006). Computer-supported collaborative learning: An historical perspective. In R. Sawyer (ed), *Cambridge handbook of the learning sciences* (pp 409–426). Cambridge University Press.

Steinmueller, W. (2017). Science fiction and innovation: A response. *Research Policy*, 46(3), 550–553.

Stevens, K., Guo, X. and Li, Y. (2018). Typology and hierarchy of students' motivations to use technology in learning. *Australasian Journal of Information Systems*, 22. [Online], https://doi.org/10.3127/ajis.v22i0.1492

Strauss, A. and Corbin, J. (1990). *Basics of qualitative research*. SAGE.

Subramaniam, M.M., Ahn, J., Fleischmann, K.R. and Druin, A. (2012). Reimagining the role of school libraries in STEM education: Creating hybrid spaces for exploration. *The Library Quarterly*, 82(2), 161–182.

Supriyadi, T., Julia, J., Aeni, A.N. and Sumarna, E. (2020). Action research in hadith literacy: A reflection of hadith learning in the digital age. *International Journal of Learning, Teaching and Educational Research*, 19(5), 99–124.

Sutton, R.I. and Staw, B.M. (1995). What theory is not. *Administrative Science Quarterly*, 40(3), 371–384.

Swan, K. and Ice, P. (2010) Special issue on the community of inquiry framework: Ten years later. *The Internet and Higher Education*, 13(1–2), 1–100.

Swedberg, R. (2012). Theorizing in sociology and social science: Turning to the context of discovery. *Theory and Society*, 41(1), 1–40.

Swedberg, R. (2016). Before theory comes theorizing or how to make social science more interesting. *The British Journal of Sociology*, 67(1), 5–22.

Tamim, R.M., Bernard, R.M., Borokhovski, E., Abrami, P.C. and Schmid, R.F. (2011). What forty years of research says about the impact of technology on learning: A second-order meta-analysis and validation study. *Review of Educational Research*, 81(1), 4–28.

Tannen, D. (1991). *You just don't understand: Women and men in conversation*. Virago.

Taylor, F. (1911). *The principles of scientific management*. Harper & Brothers.

Teague, D., Lister, R. and Ahadi, A. (2015). Mired in the web: Vignettes from Charlotte and other novice programmers. Australasian Computing Education Conference, Sydney, Australia, 27– 30 January 2015.

Teo, T. and Milutinovic, V. (2015). Modelling the intention to use technology for teaching mathematics among pre-service teachers in Serbia. *Australasian Journal of Educational Technology*, 31(4), 363–380.

Thomas, A. (2005). Children online: Learning in a virtual community of practice. *E-Learning and Digital Media*, 2(1), 27–38.

Thomas, G. (2016). *How to do your case study*. SAGE.

Toffler, A. (1980). *The third wave: The classic study of tomorrow*. Bantam.

Tondeur, J., Van Braak, J., Ertmer, P.A. and Ottenbreit-Leftwich, A. (2017). Understanding the relationship between teachers' pedagogical beliefs and technology use in education: A systematic review of qualitative evidence. *Educational Technology Research and Development*, 65(3), 555–575.

Torgerson, C. (2003). *Systematic reviews*. Continuum Books.

Tou, N.X., Kee, Y.H., Koh, K.T., Camiré, M. and Chow, J.Y. (2020). Singapore teachers' attitudes towards the use of information and communication technologies in physical education. *European Physical Education Review*, 26(2), 481–494.

TTA (1998). *The use of ICT in subject teaching: Expected outcomes for teachers*. Teacher Training Agency and the Department of Education London.

Turkle, S. (2005). *The second self: Computers and the human spirit*. MIT Press.

Turvey, M.T. (1992). Affordances and prospective control: An outline of the ontology. *Ecological Psychology*, 4(3), 173–187.

Tyack, D. and Cuban, L. (1995). *Tinkering toward utopia: A century of public school reform*. Harvard University Press.

Underwood, J. (2004). Research into information and communications technologies: Where now? *Technology, Pedagogy and Education*, 13(2), 135–145.

Valsiner, J. (1997). *Culture and the development of children's action: A theory of human development* (2nd edn). John Wiley & Sons.

Venkatesh, V., Morris, M., Davis, G. and Davis, F. (2003). User acceptance of information technology: Toward a unified view. *MIS Quarterly*, 27(3), 425–478.

Vygotsky, L.S. and Cole, M. (1978). *Mind in society: The development of higher psychological processes*. Harvard University Press.

Wajcman, J. (2010). Feminist theories of technology. *Cambridge Journal of Economics*, 34(1), 143–152.

Watson, D.M. (2001). Pedagogy before technology: Re-thinking the relationship between ICT and teaching. *Education and Information Technologies*, 6(4), 251–266.

Webb, M. (2008). Impact of IT on science education. In J. Voogt and G. Knezek (eds), *International handbook of information technology in primary and secondary education* (pp 133–148). Springer.

Wenger, E. (1998). *Communities of practice: Learning, meaning, and identity*. Cambridge University Press.

Wieland, K. (2012). Asynchronous learning networks. In N.M. Seel (ed), *Encyclopedia of the sciences of learning* (pp 345–348). Springer.

Wijetunga, D. (2014). The digital divide objectified in the design: Use of the mobile telephone by underprivileged youth in Sri Lanka. *Journal of Computer-Mediated Communication*, 19(3), 712–726.

Williamson, B. (2017). *Big Data in education: The digital future of learning, policy and practice*. SAGE.

Williamson, D., Squire, K., Halverson, R. and Gee, J. (2005). Video games and the future of learning. *Phi Delta Kappan*, 87(2), 104–111.

Wilmot, K. (2021). Learning how to theorize in doctoral writing: A tool for teaching and learning. In C.M. Winberg and S. McKenna and K. Wilmot (eds), *Building knowledge in higher education: Enhancing teaching and learning with legitimation code theory* (pp 126–142). Routledge.

Wilson, A., Watson, C., Thompson, T.L., Drew, V. and Doyle, S. (2017). Learning analytics: Challenges and limitations. *Teaching in Higher Education*, 22(8), 991–1007.

Winch, P. (2007). *The idea of a social science*. Routledge and Kegan Paul.

Xin, C. (2012). A critique of the community of inquiry framework. *Journal of Distance Education*, 26(1), 1–15.

Xue, E., Li, J. and Xu, L. (2020). Online education action for defeating COVID-19 in China: An analysis of the system, mechanism and mode. *Educational Philosophy and Theory*, 54(16), 799–811.

Yasnitsky, A. (2018). *Vygotsky: An intellectual biography*. Routledge.

Ylijoki, O.-H. (2001). Master's thesis writing from a narrative approach. *Studies in Higher Education*, 26(1), 21–34.

Yueh, H.-P. and Chiang, F.-K. (2020). AI and robotics in reshaping the dynamics of learning. *British Journal of Educational Technology*, 51(5), 1804–1807.

Zhang, J., Scardamalia, M., Reeve, R. and Messina, R. (2009). Designs for collective cognitive responsibility in knowledge-building communities. *The Journal of the Learning Sciences*, 18(1), 7–44.

Zuboff, S. (2019). *The age of surveillance capitalism: The fight for a human future at the new frontier of power*. Profile Books.

Index